Islam and “Scientific” Economics

Hasan Gürak

Islam and "Scientific" Economics

In the Pursuit of a New Paradigm

PL ACADEMIC RESEARCH

Bibliographic Information published by the Deutsche Nationalbibliothek
The Deutsche Nationalbibliothek lists this publication in the Deutsche Nationalbibliografie; detailed bibliographic data is available in the internet at http://dnb.d-nb.de.

Library of Congress Cataloging-in-Publication Data
Gürak, Hasan.
Islam and scientific economics : in the pursuit of a new paradigm / Hasan Gürak. – 1 [edition].
pages cm
ISBN 978-3-631-65492-7
1. Islam–Economic aspects. 2. Economics–Religious aspects–Islam. 3. Economic development–Religious aspects–Islam. I. Title.
BP173.75.G87 2014
330.1–dc23

2014023710

Cover illustration: © Ebru Erman

ISBN 978-3-631-65492-7 (Print)
E-ISBN 978-3-653-04766-0 (E-Book)
DOI 10.3726/ 978-3-653-04766-0

Internationaler Verlag der Wissenschaften
Frankfurt am Main 2014

PL Academic Research is an Imprint of Peter Lang GmbH.

Peter Lang – Frankfurt am Main · Bern · Bruxelles · New York · Oxford · Warszawa · Wien

This publication has been peer reviewed.

www.peterlang.com

Preface

The purpose of the book is to present the main Islamic concepts and the "scientific" foundations of "Islamic economics".

Why "scientific Islamic economics"?

Presumably the subject "Islamic economics" is of interest to any economist. To be more specific, subjects such as Islamic Banking and the interest-free economic system are rather intriguing for the pluralist minded scholar. Having had a Western "style" economics education in Sweden but, nevertheless, as a hard line antagonist and critic of mainstream economic theories, I could not overcome my intellectual curiosity to find out what really is different in Islamic economics from the Western system and to what extent it differs. However, after a short while, and to my surprise, I found out that Islamic "scientific" economic theories I was looking for, did not actually exist. Not even a universal Islamic economic theory on the subject of "interest" applicable to all nations, Muslim or non-Muslim, has been developed. Yet, "interest" is probably the most frequently discussed subject in Islamic economics. All ideas or discussions extant on the subject of interest in the Islamic economic system indicates that it was founded on the four Suras of the Holy Book, the Koran, or on the Sunnahs, which are the sayings and practices of the Prophet Mohammed. There appear not to be any "scientific" explanations or analyses.

The Holy sources may be more than sufficient for Muslims but what about non-Muslims? Is it unfair to expect that Islamic "scientific" economic theories should be applicable to, or able to guide non-Muslims, as well?

The absence of any "scientific" Islamic economic theories led me to change my primary aim, one of collating and editing the relevant Islamic "scientific" works, to one of developing a personal and critical evaluation of the present state of Islamic economics. So my initial purpose had to be changed from one of "understanding" the available literature on Islamic "scientific" economics, to one of analyzing and commenting, and even attempting to develop "new" theories in accordance with Islamic values. The fruits of my labors have resulted in this book.

There is no individual, institution or academic unit to whom I owe a debt of gratitude to; except for those researchers from whose works I have benefitted in the writing of this book. This was a great disappointment to me because I had high hopes that my "conservative" or "liberal" minded colleagues would show some interest in this work and would contribute by sharing their views. But my hopes were in vain! All the ideas presented in the book whether they are beneficial or deficient are solely my own ideas and contributions.

The only person I owe gratitude to is "Hakim John Lee" from Bodrum-Turgutreis who not only contributed by correcting my mistakes in English but also, now and then, suggested some valuable remarks which should, in fact, have come from my colleagues in the first place. Thank you Hakim!

Finally: I would ask the reader to note that almost all translations from Turkish to English were made by me. I do not claim to be a professional translator. As a result there may be, in fact, there must be errors for which I feel obliged to apologize to the authors of the original texts. The intention was sincere, though the outcome may not be in exact compliance with their original meaning.

Hasan Gürak

Table of Contents

The Islamic economic paradigm with its new and alternative scientific Islamic economic theories have to be so '**comprehensive**' as well as so perfect in the sense of '**fairness**', '**ethical values**' and '**fruitfulness**', so that when you take out the word 'Islamic', it should appeal to all societies and countries equally, regardless of their religious persuasion.

Hasan Gürak

"Neither is religious faith an alternative to scientific knowledge, nor is scientific knowledge an alternative to religious faith."

H. Gürak

Introduction

The main purpose of the three monotheistic religions based upon their ethical teachings is to provide guidelines for the individual and the community to keep them from committing sins and to regulate their behavior in accordance with their holy values in such a way that they will eventually achieve a better life in the hereafter. Islam, too, demands that its believers have faith in only one God (Allah) and live according to the tenets of Islam. **In an Islamic society, it is ethics that dominates and determines all its behavior, including its 'economic behavior'.**

Every individual has certain rights as well as duties to fulfill as ordained by Islamic tenets. These individual rights and duties ought not to be neglected under any circumstances. For example, how an individual is expected to behave in his daily life, or what conditions have to be taken into consideration in trading activities, or which items are 'Halal', (permissible), or 'Haram', (prohibited), amongst other things, are in many cases predetermined and described in detail in Islam's holy book, The Koran.

If the Koran does not express any instructions with regard to any societal event, then reference is made to a secondary source; the **Sunnah**, which is a compilation of the sayings and practices of the Prophet Muhammad. If it is the case that no ruling or explanation can be found in the Koran or in the Sunnah, a third source is invoked. These are the rulings, judgments or explanations of the **Ulama**. This is a body of religious judges who are experts on the Islamic body of law, the Sharia. The conclusions arrived at in this way are referred to as '**Ijtihad**', which are new Islamic "man-made" rulings or explanations based on the consensus of opinion amongst these Islamic judges. It is no surprise that such man-made laws could display a wide range of opinions based on the specific sectarian beliefs of the judges.

Another type of man-made law is called '**Ijma**' which implies the consensus of 'all' Islamic judges on the "rightness" of a belief or practice, as distinct from the '**Ijtihad**' which obviously displays a sectarian bias. According to a 15th century Turkish (Ottoman) religious leader Molla Hüsrev:

> *"The condition of 'ijma' is that the 'mujtahideen' living in the same century must unanimously agree... An 'ijma' bearing the necessary condition implies knowledge (science) and those who reject it shall be accused of blasphemy." (Koca; 2008; 150).*

After the period of the four Caliphs (Abu-Bakr, Omar, Usman and Ali), the Islamic scholars, or to be more specific, the Islamic judges have had a highly influential and authoritarian role in the lives of Muslims. For centuries they determined, to significant extent, the daily practices as well as any potential future developments. One of the main reasons for this was the need to expound the verses in Koran and the Sunnahs of the Prophet to people who were largely uneducated. Another reason was the need to guide the people in accordance with Islamic principles when there was no reference to a specific case in the Koran or the Sunnah. The latter reason is of significant importance because as mankind climbs the developmental ladder exposure to an ever increasing pool of global knowledge, many previously unknown problems arose which needed to be resolved in line with Islamic principles. Under such circumstances, the faithful Muslim's primarily source of consultation has been the Islamic judges.

It would be unrealistic to assume that all the opinions, interpretations or rulings of the Islamic judges have been "perfect", especially on economic matters. That is simply because; they frequently did not possess the required qualifications on these matters. In fact, even if they had the required qualifications, their interpretations, comments, and opinions would in all likelihood have been essentially different due to their subjective perception of matters not directly referred to in the Koran or Sunnahs.

On the State of Knowledge

Unfortunately the average level of qualifications of the labor force and the global competitive level of enterprises in the Islamic countries lags far behind contemporary standards in terms of their knowledge of the patenting of new ideas in the areas of technology and science. In the last four centuries, most of the scientific and technological advances have taken place in non-Islamic countries. It does not appear that this trend is likely to change in the near future. But once upon a time, the Islamic countries and their scholars were superior to their Western counterparts in science and technology. The Western Christian countries successfully transferred massive scientific and technological knowledge from Islamic countries and then developed this knowledge further. Thus, the scientific and technological development of the Western countries owes a significant debt to the scholars of Islam.

So, what prevented the Islamic countries and their scholars from further advancing the science and technology they possessed? Did they lose their mental skills and talents?

Of course they didn't! The Islamic countries and their scholars did "not" lose their mental skills or talents. But they did not do, or could not do, what was necessary in order to further develop this knowledge due to the circumstances at the time. Or, at least, they weren't as successful as the Western world in their efforts to further develop the existing science and technology.

The most significant and influential factor in this lack of development was the structure of the education system in Islamic countries. If they could have provided a successful educational system encouraging development in the positive sciences and technology, the process of development and the present situation of Islamic countries would have been a lot different from what it is today[1]. Islamic scholars, the labor force and the ordinary people would be better endowed with the proper knowledge to follow the most recent scientific and technological developments, which in turn would lead to the creation of new technologies or the discovery of new facts in the positive sciences. At least, the development gap between the Western Christian countries and the Islamic countries would be narrower that it is today.

Until recently, the educational system in the Medrese (the Islamic school) was based predominantly on the teaching of the tenets of Islam. Non-religious education was ignored. Being a "good Muslim" was the primary if not, the only, goal of the Islamic education system for centuries. Some weak attempts to challenge this approach were not successful. Ihsanoglu states with regard to the scientific and technological development during the 600 years of the Turkish Ottoman Empire; "**… the Western idea of controlling nature through science and technology was unknown for the Ottoman scholars because of their convictions based on Islam**." (Ihsanoğlu; 1996; 28). Word was that; "**new inventions were prohibited**[2]."

---

1 For a detailed analysis of the role of "knowledge in development" see H.Gürak, 2012, Economics.

2 Original version in Turkish: "Nev icat haramdır."

In the past, Islamic scholars once had a multi-dimensional education system and the natural sciences such as physics and astronomy were considered as a part of the "Philosophical thinking and teaching" curriculum in the Medrese. But, due to religious ideological differences among Islamic scholars, a strong opposition emerged against the philosophical subjects. As time passed, these opponents gained ground and eventually the study of "philosophy" became an "undesired" subject in the Medrese education system.

For example, about 1,000 years ago, the positive science subjects such as physics, chemistry and astronomy were the favored subjects in the "philosophical thinking" curriculum. Islamic philosophers of the time had a great interest in these subjects and developed many original ideas which made a serious contribution to the further development of science. But, as time passed the attitude towards philosophy and the philosophers changed and some Islamic scholars began to criticize these philosophers relentlessly. This negative attitude grew rapidly gaining support from rulers who preferred to have loyal and totally obedient subjects. After all, the ruler was considered as a person "chosen" by Allah and Allah must be obeyed totally! So must his regents on earth!

The thoughts of the well-known Turkish philosopher İbn Sina (known as **Avicenna** in the West) were denounced as an "**enemy of Islam**" and he himself was named an "**infidel**" by these opponents of philosophy who harshly criticized and unfairly judged him (Boer; 1960; 111-112). According to one opponent's remarks:

> *"It is useful that a man works on 'Fiqh' the Islamic law which is his nurture. But, philosophy could be a fatal poison; because the man would be open to doubt and might easily lose faith." (Boer; 1960; 111-112).*

It is said that:

> *"(What)... Sharia stands for is prerogative, while philosophy which opposes it, stands for superstition" (Bolay; 1993; 24).*

These anti-philosophy centered Islamic scholars actually prevented the development of;

> *"... philosophical and speculative thought under the guidance of (a) free and liberal intellect" (Sayar; 2009; 69).*

As a consequence, the opportunity of catching up with the contemporary developments in secular scientific areas was hindered.

On the "Creative" Mental Skills of Man

All the arguments, definitions, comments and criticism in this book are the subjective views of the author. They are definitely not divine revelations or "perfect" views; therefore they are bound to be "imperfect" and contain some shortcomings. Thus they are open to all kinds of criticism. As a matter of fact, everybody searching for "alternative" approaches to conventional issues and who aims to contribute to the emergence of a new paradigm is liable to criticism, some of which is expected to be relentless and some constructive. This is an inevitable outcome of daring to "buck the system". Therefore, it is imperative that the reader keep an "open-mind" and a "tolerant" viewpoint in order for him or her to make a "fair" and "unbiased" judgment on the "unconventional" views presented. After all, the author is using the mental abilities granted by the Creator, these are human qualities which by their very nature cannot be "perfect". My sole purpose in this book is an attempt to look into the issues but not to denigrate the sources from which they came.

Let's analyze the concept of an "Allah given mental ability". It is widely acknowledged that the only way human beings can to develop new ideas is making use of their mental abilities. For the faithful, these mental abilities are granted by the Creator and their quality and extent varies from individual to individual. During the historical process, mankind has developed countless new ideas by utilizing this mental ability. The degree of utilization is reflected in the development level of societies. Some countries are intellectually poorer, and some richer.

Many new ideas are opposed by the status quo; sometimes indulgently, sometimes relentlessly, as in the case of Galileo. But the opposition can change over time. In fact, it frequently does and even takes on a complimentary form. Being open-minded and tolerant to "new ideas" is not only ethical but, is in fact, a human virtue.

"New ideas" may not always produce desirable results or they may be incorrect or inadequate. No matter how it originates, a new idea makes some impact on society and paves the way for further development or lead to other new ideas. For example, if there was no contribution from the "relatively less knowledgeable" astronomers in the 11th, 12th, 13th, 14th and 15th Centuries, Galileo or Newton would not have had a pool of knowledge to draw on and build their more sophisticated theories. If there was no "relatively" less developed contributions by Newton, then there would not be the more sophisticated ideas of Einstein. A similar logic is applicable to all disciplines. For example, if there was no contributions by the "relatively less knowledgeable" economists like Ibn Haldun and others, A. Smith and D. Ricardo would not have been able to further develop their ideas on economics.

On the "New Knowledge" on Economics

Creating new ideas is an ability not granted to any other creature but man. Since man is created by Allah as his vicegerent on earth superior to all other creatures due to his distinctive mental abilities, there should be no problem with using these Allah-given abilities. In fact, we can take a step further and suggest that man "has to" use his distinctive Allah-given mental abilities, as the vicegerent of Allah.

From this perspective, having a say on worldly matters is not the privilege of one individual or a group of individuals, whether it be on scientific or metaphysical matters. It is the privilege of all men; **having "new ideas" about Islamic economics is no exception**. So, any man endowed with the mental ability and appropriate background may develop "new" and/or "alternative" ideas in the field of Islamic economics on matters not clearly specified in the Koran or in Hadith. Since the knowledge developed by man is not the "absolute truth", all kinds of "conventional" ideas, including those on Islamic economics, should be open to criticism and revaluation. After all, we know that the more we learn about the things around us, the more we realize how little we really know!

The Prophet is once reported to have said; "**one should not hesitate even going to China to learn new knowledge**." Taking into account the transportation facilities of that time and the distances involved, the importance of learning could not have been put more clearly. Therefore, Muslims have to be open-minded and encourage the development of "new ideas" in any scientific field.

The Content and the Method

It is important for the non-Muslim world to understand "Islamic economics" for many reasons. For example, Islamic economists claim that Islamic economic system differs essentially and radically from any other system; it is neither "capitalistic" as practiced in the Western countries nor is it "socialistic". The Suras of the Holy Koran emerges as the principle source of all economic behavior and practices which are subject to the commands of Allah as they are stated in Koran. A faithful Muslim has no choice but to live according to Koran's principles.

The purpose of the book is to discuss the main concepts and theoretical foundations of the so called "Islamic economics". The study will attempt to outline the major features of "Islamic economics" which are claimed to be different from the so called 'Western' economics.

Since Islam is a "universal" religion, I had expected to find universal "Islamic scientific economic theories" which would apply "universally". However, to my surprise, there were no such economic theories. In fact, there was not even a theory about "interest", the most frequently cited subject in the Islamic economic system. This seemed to be a serious omission.

In the absence of Islamic "scientific" economic theories developed by the Islamic economists, there was no choice but to change the purpose and the method of study. The new purpose is to evaluate the present condition of Islamic economics in terms of existing "scientific" economic theories and to present some "un-traditional" analyses and new approaches. To serve this purpose, the first three chapters are designed to evaluate and discuss the present "scientific" state of Islamic economics and make, now and then, some references or comparisons to Western economic theories. In other words, the first three chapters are concerned with the "scientific" economic theories, analysis and comments.

In the fourth section, an "**alternative**" **value-price theory** is introduced which is different from the mainstream "blackboard" doctrines but in compliance with Islamic values and principles. Its content was published before in a slightly different form without making any reference to Islamic values or principles. In this section, there are somewhat minor differences but essentially the analysis is the same. The purpose is to contribute to the development of an **Islamic value-price theory** which is the basis of all economic theories.

The fifth section concerns trade activities (domestic and global). It we know the Prophet had made his living by trade before the time of his Divine Revelation by the Angel Gabriel. But surprisingly, there has not been any "**scientific**" **trade theory** developed by Islamic economists displaying the pros and cons of trade **for Muslims or non-Muslims**. Maybe some economists take this omission into consideration and start building "alternative" and globally valid **Islamic trade theories**.

The sixth section discusses the most frequently cited subject in Islamic economics; the "**interest**". In this section interest (or "**surplus**" or "**additional payment**") is evaluated from the perspective of "**earned income**" in conjunction with the **labor effort and risk assumed** in the supply of goods or services.

The principle sources of reference for this study, as in all Islamic economic studies, are firstly, the Holy Book, the Koran and secondly, the Sunnah (the sayings and practices of the Prophet). However, since our subject matter is "scientific" economics and neither Koran nor the Sunnah are scientific economic textbooks, we made an effort to present some different arguments by using "**Allah's gift to mankind; our mental abilities**". Our purpose is to make a humble contribution to the further development of Islamic "scientific" economics.

Chapter-1

Revaluation of Islamic Economics-1
Developing Islamic Economic Theories

"In Islamic society, it is ethics that dominates economics and not the other way around."

Naqvi, 1981, Ethics and Economics

Introduction

Initially, the purpose of this book was to analyze the 'scientific' economic theories built upon the Islamic faith. As Muslims know, Islam is the last divine 'universal' religion bestowed on mankind. The Islamic economic order is vehemently defended by a group of experts called the 'Ulama' which is comprised of Islamic scholars. Consequently Islamic economists should have a knowledge of "universal scientific" economic theories which should be applicable not only to Islamic countries but also to people of other faiths, be they Christians, Jews, Buddhists or even to those who do not subscribe to any faith at all. Thus, having detailed information and knowledge about such a system should become not only a useful tool but an economic necessity.

However, an unforeseen factor emerged as the study progressed; there were no alternative Islamic 'scientific' economic' theories to replace or even to challenge the 'universally' (?) applicable scientific theories developed by Western economists. There was not even ANY alternative 'scientific' economic theory about the interest rate which is the most favorite economic issue cited by the Ulama and other Islamic economists. Nor is there any economic theory about the Islamic financial system. The Ulama's and Islamic economists' remarks, comments or instructions on interest rate related issues were, in general, those which were based on the verses of the Holy Koran and Sunnahs, (the sayings and practices of the Prophet Muhammad, as they have been observed for hundreds of years). As such, they were, inevitably, highly influenced by religious ethics and moral issues.

Zakat, (which is an obligatory tax levied on the wealth and not on the income, of every Muslim and Islamic institution and which directly affects income distribution), is one of the most frequently discussed topics in Islamic economics after the interest rate. As yet, there has been no scientific economic analysis of, or theory proposed on this issue. The same situation applies also for the **Waqf** (which is an Islamic foundation) which plays a significant role in the functioning of the Islamic economic order. It seems reasonable to suggest that, Islamic economists should have developed some form of theory and an analytical method at least on one of these key issues which differs significantly from a Western understanding of these concepts and institutions. In fact, these Islamic concepts, theories and/or institutions should have been put into practice and further developed a long time ago, in order to display the 'superiority' of Islamic economics over those of the non-Muslim world, as is proclaimed by the Ulama and other Islamic economists.

Although it is difficult to admit, it is undeniable that the 'scientific' contributions of Islamic economists are even less satisfactory in other related fields of economics. For example, up to now there is still no value-price theory, growth theory or an income distribution theory based upon Islamic principles.

Islamic Economic Theories in Retrospect

Historically, in regard to economic issues, we know that the Ulama (Islamic scholars) have always been the most competent and the most influential persons because they are able to introduce the "Fatwa". The primary source of these judgments or rulings has always been the Koran, the holy book of Islam. The secondary source has been the Sunnahs, i.e., the sayings and practices of the Prophet Muhammad. If there is no reference to an economic issue, either in the Koran or in a Sunnah, then the Ulama used to formulate a ruling known as 'Ijtihad' or interpretation. This provided a new rule from the recognized sources of Shariah, i.e., the Islamic law. But, these rulings have never been transformed into economic theories from which, not only Muslim but also non-Muslim countries and their citizens, could benefit. These Islamic theories could, for instance, attempt to reveal the negative effects of interest rate on an economy in the non-Muslim world by using Islamic economic principles.

One of the reasons for not developing Islamic economic theories for the non-Muslim world may be the assumption that the world population will convert to Islam in a future time so then they will benefit from the principles of the Islamic economy. As a result of this type of thinking there might be no motivation to convince non-Muslims about Islamic economics because they will soon be Muslims anyway. Maybe the reason for this neglect is the inadequacy or incompetence of Islamic scholars who have had the final say on Islamic laws and practices in the past centuries. Maybe both of these reasons are valid, or there might be other explanations.

Whatever the reasons for this neglect might be, the fact is there are NO Islamic economic theories. Given this fact, it is now time to consider what can be done to bridge this gap. For example; should Islamic scholars, as they did in the past, play the determinant role, with regard to all economic matters, in the developing of Islamic economic theories? Or should the gap be bridged by experts in the economics sciences? What is the potential for non-Muslim economists to contribute to the emergence of 'universally' or 'globally' applicable economic theories? Who should evaluate Islamic economic theories and what should the procedure be?

Probably the most critical issue for economists in their attempt to develop 'new and alternative' Islamic economic theories would be the likelihood that they would be in contravention of the decisions or the thinking of the Ulama, the Islamic scholars. For many Islamic economists, accepting the rulings of the Ulama on economic matters would be rather convenient. Thus, they would avoid the serious problem of being in contravention of the rulings of the Ulama. After all, who would dare to question the rulings of the Ulama based on their interpretations of Islamic law?

On the other hand, a related and critical question arises: How appropriate and wise is it to allow the Ulama who frequently do not possess sufficient qualifications which allow them to make rulings about the complex economic affairs of present day societies? The question here is one of expertise. Do the Ulama have the required level of knowledge about today's complex economic situations? The reader should duly note that Islamic law, which is the true domain of the Ulama, is not an issue here. The area of expertise of the Ulama is the interpretation of Islamic law. And the area of expertise of the economists is the interpretation and application of the laws of economics.

As expressed before, the primary purpose of this paper is to present contributions on economic theories which are considered to be substantially Islamic. But, these contributions do not appear to exist; at least not to my knowledge. Under these circumstances, what can be done? Rationally, scholars will have to come up with some "alternative" economic theories. Another rational approach would be, as M.A. Mannan pointed out, there shouldn't be any problem in adapting present institutions or practices of the capitalist or socialist systems if they prove to be useful (Mannan; 28).

The prominent Islamic scholar Ibn Qayyim shared a similar view to M.A. Mannan. According to Ibn Qayyim there is no need for the approval of the Koran for the legality of any politics. "**The fact of not being disapproved is sufficient**." (Apaydın: in Demir, Ed., 1999; 87).

Islam and Economic Knowledge

Economics can be defined as a social study of the relationships of production, distribution, and exchange, between individuals, communities, firms, and countries. It also aims to find remedies for the related problems and to forecast future projections. There are 'no permanent resolutions' or 'absolute truths' in economics. There are too many independent variables which can affect economic outcomes. Would it really be logical to expect to find from such an indeterminate and "slippery" social science as economics any reliable facts that comply with a 'faith' based on the Islamic belief?

Once upon a time, religious teachings and their dogmas were, at least, as influential in the lives of individuals in Christian countries as they are in Islamic countries today. However, over time, the economic ideologies, especially the neoclassical ideology, managed to leave any kind of religious, emotional, cultural and historical influence completely outside the realm of economic theories. The "religious" man was gone and replaced by 'Homo Economicus', a fictitious individual who behaved like a robot, free from the influence of any historical, cultural or psychological changes. Now, economic science had individuals without any religious influence or humanitarian values.

However, in Islam everything is exactly the opposite. An economic system with out religious values and principles are unthinkable. A Muslim has no choice but to live in accordance with Islamic principles in every sense of the meaning, from daily prayers to buying, selling, eating, living, etc. Although the Holy Koran is not a textbook of economics, Islamic scholars have always been highly influential on the economic practices of Muslims which must always be in compliance with Islamic teaching. The Islamic principles and its associated rules are, according to M. Sadr, the doctrine of Islamic economics which is the method pursued to solve the economic problems in the daily life of the Muslim society (Sadr; 1980; 12). For Sadr a society without an economic methodology is unthinkable. That is because; every society makes an attempt to accumulate wealth and to distribute it. In order to organize such practices, it needs a method which is suitable for its own infrastructure. This methodology determines the rules of that society's economic life.

Nowadays, the concept of "Islamic economics" is well-known, even amongst non-Muslims. People all around the world are, to some degree, familiar with it. Islamic financial institutions have been coexisting and competing with the Western financial institutions for many decades. Not surprisingly, they have been constantly increasing their business volume.

Though the non-Muslim world is getting used to some of the Islamic practices, the concept of Islamic economics as such is still, for many, a dubious concept and many aspects are in need of explanation and clarification. In other words, many Islamic economists, unlike their non-Islamic counterparts, do not seem to have agreed on the meaning of many key concepts. For example, though a large percentage of the Islamic economists and scholars seem to refute the concept of 'interest rate' as un-Islamic, others argue that it is not clear what 'type' of interest rate is forbidden by the Koran. To them, for example, an interest rate equal to the inflation rate should be considered permissible. The characteristics that distinguish Islamic economics from the Western style capitalist or socialist economic systems are yet another area open to debate.

For many economists with a Western education in economics, Islamic economics is a slightly different version of capitalism. This view is strongly opposed by both the Islamic economists and Islamic scholars, who claim that Islamic economics is essentially neither capitalist nor socialist. It is simply 'Islamic economics' which is ethical, more egalitarian and fairer than other types of economics. In Turkey, there exists yet another angle to this dispute. Many Turkish Islamic economists, when they speak or write use the expression, 'The Economics of Islam' (Islam Ekonomisi) as if Islam describes or suggests a specific type of economic knowledge. Islamic economists have to sort out these kinds of identity problems as soon as possible, if they aim to be better understood by the non-Islamic economists.

Influence of Islamic Scholars on Economic Issues

There is a critical aspect of Islamic economics that should not be overlooked. According to the Islamic faith, the complete and full adaptation and implementation of Islamic economic principles can only be realized in Islamic societies governed totally in accordance with Islamic principles. To put it another way, proper Islamic economics can only flourish in those societies organized according to Islamic values. In the case when such a society does not exist, then Muslims should pursue an Islamic life style which is in accordance with the values of the society in which they live. For example, faithful Muslims have to learn how to comply with non-Muslim regulations.

The rulers of the countries such as Iran, Pakistan, and Saudi Arabia claim that their people live in an Islamic country run by the Islamic principles of the Koran. However, such self-proclamations do not mean much in reality and some claim that their life in these countries is not in full compliance with Koranic teachings.

Some Islamic scholars refer to the period ruled by the Prophet Muhammad (610-632) as the true Islamic period during which Islamic teachings were fully implemented. Some scholars add to this the period under the rule of four Caliphs, Abu Bakr, Omar, Usman and Ali (between 632 and 661A.D.). Yet, this is a rather short period in the history of Muslims; only 51 years. The ideal period under the rule of Prophet Muhammad is even shorter, only 22 years. It should be borne in mind that the first 12 years in Mecca, under the rule of the Prophet, was not without its troubles, including the 10 years he had to spend in Medina. Within this time context, the 'ideal' period of full Islamic rule appears rather short.

About 1360 years has passed since the period of last Caliph and many things have changed radically since then. The knowledge level of individuals, the level of technological development, production relationships, social relationships, the institutions, the expectations of individuals have all changed. Nor are the economic problems the same as they were 1360 years ago. However, over the same period of time the influential position of the Islamic scholars on economic issues does not seem to have changed.

In his book titled 'Mentality and Religion', S. Ülgener (2006) notes:

> *"Throughout history, religion has been influencing the entire life style ranging from family relations to the various strata of society, politics, and artistic values; sometimes successfully and sometimes unsuccessfully; but always intervening with the claim to be an organizer." (Ülgener-b; 2006; 8)*

Therefore, in the Islamic world this practice of continued consultation with Islamic scholars is motivated by a desire to intervene and determine economic issues. This practice has not diminished in modern times; on the contrary, it still plays an important role in the life of many believers. As an inevitable consequence of this practice, Islamic scholars, or to be more specific, the scholars of Islamic law, still enjoy a highly influential role in almost every economic matter and relationship in Islamic countries or in the Islamic enclaves in other countries.

However, the success of the opinions of Islamic scholars on some economic matters, especially with regard to the level of industrialization and technological progress seems to be dubious or, at least, limited. If, the so called Islamic countries or countries where the Muslim population is in the majority, have not been successful in transforming their societies to 'advanced' countries, producing high-technology goods and services as they have in the developed Western part of the world, then it is not only the rulers of these countries but also the opinion of the Islamic scholars, influencing a wide range of social issues, who should be open to criticism. According to a widely respected Islamic belief; a Muslim should always strive to gain 'knowledge', even if it is in a distant part of the world. This belief led to a level of advancement and improvement in Islamic societies which lifted them to more advanced level than their Western counterparts in the 11th, 12th and 13th Centuries. However Islamic countries and their societies have failed to follow up on the technological development stage of the contemporary Western countries. They presently lag far behind in regard to producing an 'advanced' level of technology or science.

An interesting fact about 'some' of the modern Islamic people is their high admiration for the Western capitalist lifestyle and their aspirations to live in those non-Muslim countries. If they somehow get an opportunity to go to these countries, they do not hesitate to lie about, denigrate, or attempt to humiliate their home country, just to get a residence permit. Yet, according to common Islamic teachings, the people in the developed capitalist countries pursue an extravagant lifestyle, are driven by an excessive passion for "consumer-ism" and greed. Such behavior is against the basic principles of Islam and is gravely sinful. Why, then, are" faithful" Muslims so anxious to live in those sinful Western countries? Why are they so dissatisfied with their home countries?

Maybe some of the reasons could be:

1. The failure of their rulers to fully practice Islamic principles?
2. The citizens fail to live up to the expected Islamic values?
3. The misguided opinions and the decisions of the Islamic scholars?
4. The economic, social and political practices of the Western capitalist countries?
5. Perhaps, a combination of some or all of the above.
6. Or some other factors that we don't know about?

These questions are important questions which deserve appropriate answers.

The difference between Islamic economics and the "Others"

According to those who look forward to living in a thorough 'Islamic' society, the capitalist economic system is un-Islamic because it imposes an extravagant life-style that encourages an unbridled passion for unlimited consumption. For example, in western societies, while "greed" is encouraged, society faces many serious problems ranging from waste to poverty, pollution, and income inequality, etc. Therefore, a capitalist (Western) economic system is not considered an "appropriate" economic system for humanity; certainly not for the Muslims.

For Islamic economists and Islamic scholars, the Islamic economic system is neither capitalistic nor socialist in nature. It is an economic system with particular features. But, the question is; are these claims by the Islamic scholars and economists justified in terms of the authenticity of the Islamic economic system? Does the Islamic economic system really contain particular characteristics which essentially differ from a capitalist or socialist system? If so, what are these differences? Before we attempt to answer these questions, let's remind ourselves what capitalism or socialism is.

Capitalism is an economic system characterized by the private ownership of production and driven by the profit motive. The sole purpose of the supply of goods and services is to maximize net profit in the long-term, though there might be some other motives in the short- or medium-term. Alternatively, we can define capitalism as the economic system where production relationships are based on private property and personal interests.

Private ownership of the means of production did not emerge with the advent of capitalism. For centuries, even thousands of years, "private-owned" tools and other instruments were employed in the supply of agricultural products or commodities supplied by small scale producers (artisans). So, the private ownership argument alone cannot describe a capitalist society properly. One of the distinctive features of capitalism from these relatively less developed societies was the larger scale supply of commodities under the same roof, first in workshops, then in factories. Another and related feature was the relatively more advanced technologies used in the supply of various commodities on a large scale. At the same time, a working group of people called the "proletariat" had emerged who had nothing to sell but their labor in exchange for a wage. The share of the total value of industrial goods and services in the national income was constantly growing. But, most importantly, a new class was emerging in the society whose members were increasingly gaining more political power which they used to transform their society, from top to bottom.

At present, as far as we know there seems to be no 'pure' capitalistic economic system in which all the means of production are in private hands. What we observe generally is an economic system in which wealth and property are partly owned by private individuals, partly by the state or by non-profit institutions. This is also referred to as a 'mixed' economic system. There are, in principle, no substantial differences between a 'pure' economic system and a 'mixed' economic system as far as the interests of the private property holders are concerned. The private profit motive as the main driving force in economics exists in both systems.

One of the distinguishing features of the capitalist system is the class conflict between the workers and capitalists. As we know, there is a contrary relationship between the interests of the workers and those of the capitalists. In other words, as the proportionate share of the workers, in the net added-value rises, i.e. the real wage level rises, the net income of the capitalist declines, and vice versa.

Socialism is economic system in which the means of production is owned and run by the state on behalf of the public, though there might be some degree of private property ownership. Alternatively, socialism can be defined as an economic system organized in such a way as to give priority to the interests of the public in general, instead of the individual. Profit making is no longer the driving force of the system.

The advocates of the Islamic economic order claim that their system is different to any other. It is neither essentially capitalist nor socialist. Let us take a closer look and see how realistic this claim is.

At first glance, we see that there is a close resemblance between the Islamic and socialist economic systems with regard to placing the public's interest before individual interests. Whenever it is considered as necessary, the rulers can intervene in the functioning of the economy to protect public interests. Apart from that, there doesn't seem to be any serious resemblance to the socialist economic system. If we look at the socialist system from a religious point of view, these two systems are completely at odds with one another.

As to the resemblance(s) or difference(s) between capitalist economic system and the Islamic economic system: we can refer to the two basic features of capitalism;

1. Private ownership of the means of production.
2. The profit motive.

Regarding these two basic features, there is no difference between the Islamic economic system and capitalist economic system. Another area of resemblance is observed in the inequality, or opposing interests, with regard to the functional income distribution between the capital owners and the laborers. If the real wage rate increase is in proportion to the added-value of the product, the real profit rate would be negatively affected, that is it would decline in proportion, cet. par.

That the Islamic system resembles the capitalist economic system on such critical issues should not come as such a surprise. Islamic economics has never been hostile to private property or to making a profit; not in the past nor in the present. Inequality in the functional income as well as in household income is also a part of the Islamic economic system. Although it is not considered desirable, the advocates of Islamic economics who claim that Islamic economic system is 'different', should at least demonstrate some logical grounds to make such claims. If there are no noteworthy differences on the critical economic issues, what are the distinguishing features?

In the economic analyses, comments, explanations, forecasts and all other related issues, the major striking difference appears to be that the approaches and behavior are based on **Islamic values and principles**. Western style economics is represented by '**Homo Economicus**' who is selfish, attempts to maximize personal gain, and has no emotions. Nothing in the past influences his/her present behavior or position. She/he makes decisions like a mechanical robot. Religious values have no place in the mind or the behavior of "Homo Economicus". His/her mind should focus only on maximizing personal gain at any cost.

‘**Homo Islamicus**’, the Islamic economic man, on the other hand, displays very distinct characteristics from Homo Economics. Probably the most distinctive characteristic of Homo Islamicus is that he/she should be driven by the motive of ‘**Taqwa**’ (obedience to the rules of Islam). Regardless of the socio-economic position, whether producer or consumer, the economic behavior of the Homo Islamicus should always and everywhere fully complies with the Islamic values and principles. In other words, Homo Islamicus cannot live any way he/she desires, in order to pursue self-interest, or to produce or consume any product. Even when he/she spends personal income or wealth, the act has to be done in line with Islamic values. For example, there is no restriction on making profit, but the genuine rich Muslim has to spend his/her income in the way of Allah, which is called ‘**Infaq**’. In other words, the rich has to assume responsibility and help ‘other’ Muslims in financial distress, an obligatory behavior for all Muslims.

Accumulating savings just for the sake of saving, avoiding investment with these savings is against the Islamic faith and considered a sin. In addition, a genuine Muslim should always strive to avoid ‘excessive and unnecessary’ consumption. Thus, spending one’s income on unnecessary consumer items is against Islamic values. Another Islamic duty is to protect and to preserve the environment. Zakat, the sharing of a portion of wealth, not income, with the needy is another Islamic obligation.

Finding a genuine Homo Islamicus in contemporary societies must be, at least, as difficult as finding a genuine Homo Economicus.

Islamic economics-reconsidered

Getting back to the discussion of whether Islamic economics is different from the “others”; in view of the above discussions, would it be logical to consider Islamic economics as distinctly different from other economic systems? Does Islamic economics indeed reveal some distinct characteristics that differ from capitalism?

Yes it does!

Renowned economic scholars from Western countries do not hesitate to rename the “capitalist system” from time to time, in accordance with their ideological stand-point and nobody seems to find it strange or inappropriate. For example, the capitalist system is often referred to as the ‘market economy’ or a ‘liberal economy’. “International trade”, which has existed for thousands of years, is nowadays called ‘global’ trade. What is worthy of note is that the outcome of all these changes in nomenclature is that many economists and non-economists seem to think that we have a 'new' economic order when we use the word 'global'. They appear to be completely unaware of the ideological background of this term. Given these facts the title; 'Islamic economics' should not be considered as inappropriate. Islamic economists have every right to name their economic system in accordance with their own values or ideology.

It is not our purpose or place to evaluate or to discuss the appropriateness of Islamic economic principles in relation to Islamic religious principles. This is the task of Islamic scholars, not of economists. If Islamic economists and scholars think that the major and the distinguishing difference between Islamic economics and other types of economics is due to religious-ethical values, then one should not overlook the fact that even in the Western countries, there is a growing interest in the ethical values, if not in the religious aspects of economics. Thus, it would be a mistake to claim that ethical values are important only for Islamic economics. In fact, there is a growing convergence of ethical values. For example, sensitivity in areas such as, inequality, income distribution, extravagant consumption and environmental problems seem to be growing daily. There are perhaps more common ethical issues linking Islamic economics to the economics of some Western nations.

Given that there are both similarities and differences between Islamic economics and the 'others', the key question remains to be answered: Does Islamic economics possess the basic economic theories which are 'universally' or 'globally' applicable even to non-Muslim countries? Economic theories with "universal" (?) or global applicability are important as the Islamic economic system claims to be superior to 'other' economic systems.

Islamic Economics

An economist's perception of Islamic economics varies in accordance with her/his ideological background. Therefore, it is not surprising to encounter various types of definitions of Islamic economics. In many respects it is similar to the description of an elephant by a blind person who touches different parts of the elephant. Therefore, it would be useful to define our perception of Islamic economics in order to avoid any confusion in terminology.

As we have said, Islamic economists and scholars claim that Islamic economics is 'different' from capitalism. However from the point of view of an economist trained in a western country, there are no significant differences between Islamic economics and capitalism in regard to key issues such as profit motive and private property. Yet, Islamic economic thinking subscribes to some forms of intervention and limitations in the functioning of free markets, which have no counterpart in Western economic practice or theory. According to Asher-Wilson:

> *"The conditions come from two distinctive sources: self and state. Self-conditions emanate from the belief of the individual in the ethical code of conduct provided in the Shari"ah." (Ashker-Wilson; 2006; 399).*

U. Chapra has no objections to persons driven by the profit motive, but after drawing attention to the importance of the question of responsibility, asks this critical question:

> *"How does Islam induce individuals to pursue their self-interest within the bounds of social interest in situations where there is a conflict between self-interest and social interest?" (Chapra; 2001-a; 28).*

And he provides the answer himself:

> *"Islam tries to accomplish this task by giving self-interest a longer term perspective - stretching it beyond the span of this world into the Hereafter." (Chapra; 2001-a; 28).*

The evaluation of the correctness and appropriateness of one's actions with reference to Islamic values and principles is the concern of Islamic scholars. Having said that, we will take the utmost care to focus our attention only on Islamic 'scientific' economic theories which could be 'scientific alternatives' to Western economic theories.

Once again, we need to point out the role of Islamic values and principles in determining the outcome of economic relations. And, once again, we should remember that there are no Islamic 'scientific' economic theories which could pave the way for non-Muslim economists to follow the so called 'superior' Islamic economic system. There are certainly some definite Islamic economic opinions on economic matters such as interest rate. Yet, these opinions do seem to be more like opinions, comments or mere criticism rather than advancement in 'economic theory'. In addition, and more importantly, with regard to these 'scientific' theories, Islamic economics still lack key theories on value-price, growth, trade, income distribution, employment and inflation. A Hadith, (a saying of the Prophet Muhammad) states that the wage of an employee should be paid before the worker's sweat dries on his or her brow. Yet, there is no Islamic wage theory. Again, according to the Prophet Muhammad, nine-tenths of the material or spiritual food blessed by God originates from trade. But, surprisingly, despite the Prophet Muhammad being an accomplished trader, **Islamic economics lacks an international trade theory** (see Güler; 2012; 17).

The critical question is: What are the Islamic economists doing in order to fill in these important gaps?

The lack of a scientific dimension

According to Yousri, it is an imperative for Islamic economics to possess authentic economic theories, i.e. an Islamic economic model cannot be constituted without authentic theories.

> *"An Islamic economic theory is indispensable for comprehensive economic analysis as well as for making sound economic policies. In fact, theory in any discipline plays the most important role in its development. Islamic economics cannot develop a unique identity without having specialized theories capable of giving acceptable interpretation different phenomena and discovering the causes of the problems which face their society." (Yousri; 2013; 25).*

If an 'alternative' Islamic economic system is to be constructed, there is a need, not only for a 'general' economic theory but also a need for an Islamic micro- and macro-economic theory. And, according to Yousri, there already exists a body of 'scientific' economic knowledge.

> *"The science of Islamic economics has emerged from, and built upon, Islamic economic knowledge, which is the body of knowledge established and assembled by* Fuqha *and Muslim scholars who showed interest in the economic aspects and problems of their societies." (Yousri; in Ahmed; 2002; 21).*

The existing Islamic knowledge Yousri mentions is not in the Koran. It is the knowledge possessed by the Islamic scholars, i.e., the Ulama. Does the knowledge of Ulama indeed contain the 'scientific' economic theories we are searching for? According to our information, so far, the answer has to be 'No!' There is no sign of such 'scientific' theories. In fact, it would be unfair to expect the Ulama to fill this critical scientific gap, given the nature of the knowledge they have. The level of knowledge of contemporary economic science does not seem to have been mastered by many Islamic scholars.

On the evaluation of the appropriateness of economic relations to Islamic teachings, Yousri warns Islamic scholars, (to be more specific, the Islamic jurists):

> *"Thinking that we can depend "directly" on* Sharia'h *to formulate successful economic policies is misleading and may not only lead to failure in resolving the economic problems but perhaps would further complicate them. A crisis would arise and handicap the development of Islamic economics if Islamic jurists (*fuqha*) think that they can play the role of the economists." (Yousri; in H. Ahmed; 2002; 47-48).*

It is common knowledge that Islamic scholars since the 7th century have always been concerned with the outcome of economic relations. They have often, if not always, been the determining force in any economic relationships.

The powerful influence of the past Islamic scholars in economics can still be seen today. For example, Imam Ghazali's opinions on many economic issues are still highly respected and followed, even though he wrote these about 1,000 years ago. Many contemporary economists often quote from his works and regard his opinions as a positive example in solving present day economic problems. For example, S. Orman blesses Ghazali's economic opinions in his work 'Ghazali's Economic Philosophy' published in 2007. Yousri's remarks on the role of Islamic jurists in economics will surely annoy Mr. S. Orman and many of his cohorts.

It would be a serious mistake to describe the role Islamic scholars or jurists as outmoded. In fact, they should not feel outmoded or superfluous, at all. Yousri seems to have a new role for them:

> *"Muslim jurists (*fuqha*) who are interested in economics would best benefit the new paradigm by advising the Islamic economists on* Sharia's *rules which concern their art, reviewing their work and expressing their agreement or disagreement on the use or misuse of* Sharia's *rules in this work." (Yousri; in Ahmed; 2002; 48, footnote 23)*

Because, says Yousri:

> *"Islamic economics is not synonymous with* fiqh *rules of financial transactions, contracts and* zakat, *as some Muslim jurists think." (Yousri; in Ahmed; 2002; 57).*

Suwailem does not seem to be satisfied, either, with the present developmental level of Islamic economic theories.

> *"Despite the substantial research done by researchers in this domain over the last four decades, the progress in developing a coherent theory of Islamic economics is below expectations." (Suwailem; 2008; 81).*

Because, he thinks, the contemporary works Islamic economics seems to be under too much influence from the neoclassical economic doctrine.

Z. Hasan is another, who does not seem to be satisfied with the present developmental level of Islamic 'scientific' economics. He says:

> *"... there is a growing perception, which this author shares, that Islamization of knowledge has barely taken off the ground." (Hasan; 1989; 2).*

It is a fact that Islamic economics, or rather the Islamic economists, have been highly and extensively influenced by the mainstream neoclassical ideology. They have even attempted to build some Islamic theories using neoclassical criteria. Ahmed is one of them who says that:

> *"Tools are needed to analyze the micro-foundations of an economy on which the fundamental theories are based on. In the absence of analytical tools, study of an*

economic system becomes perplexing. Basic issues remain unanswered and consistent analysis is not possible. Lack of tools that study the micro-foundations of Islamic economic theory has failed to provide a functional alternative to the existing systems. The result is that discussions in Islamic economics have often produced "contradictory proposals and fallacious inferences." (Ahmed; in Ahmed; 2002; 125).

Thinking that Islamic economics is unsuccessful in constituting an Islamic economic paradigm is not a problem, For Ahmed as the solution is at hand; no need to search for it elsewhere.

"... even though the paradigm of an Islamic economic system is different from the neoclassical one, the basic principles of the marginalist analytical tools do not contradict Islamic principles and can be used to study the underlying behavior of agents in an Islamic system." (Ahmad; in Ahmed; 2002; 126).

Khan, who shares a similar view to Ahmed, proposes a simpler solution:

"Islamic economics can be discussed under the neoclassical framework by simply adding Islamic values to it." (in Ahmed; 2002; 126).

Islamic economists are expected to adapt an economic doctrine that dismisses all religious or ethical values, accepts the prohibited concept of interest rate, and use this ideology to build a so called Islamic 'scientific' economic theory in compliance with Islamic teachings.

Kahn and Ahmed are not alone. According to Chapra, the subject of Islamic economics is as described by the neoclassical model:

"The subject matter of all economics, irrespective of whether it is mainstream or Islamic, is the allocation and distribution of scarce resources which have unlimited uses." (Chapra; 2001-a; 11)

However, Chapra warns that, the distinctive characteristic of Islamic economics should be its appropriateness to the Islamic faith, and to the practice of religious laws and principles. Because, Islam does not find it satisfactory just to increase material wealth. Therefore, Chapra thinks a society endowed with proper Islamic institutions has to be founded and goes on to say:

"Unlike the secularist market paradigm, human well-being is not considered to be dependent primarily on maximizing wealth and consumption; it requires a balanced satisfaction of both the material and the spiritual needs of the human personality. The spiritual need is not satisfied merely by offering prayers; it also requires the moulding of individual and social behavior in accordance with the Shariah *(Islamic teachings), which is designed to ensure the realization of the* maqasid al-Shariah, *the goals of the* Shariah, *... two of the most important of which are socio-economic justice and the well-being of all God's creatures." (Chapra; 2001-a; 25).*

The path to be followed is described by Siddiqi.

> *"... the essentials of theory of Islamic economics is rooted in the Qur'an and Sunnah and the implications and implementation of these essentials are to be searched in other Islamic sources like Fiqh[3], Usool Fiqh[4], and Islamic history." (Khan; in Ahmed; 2002; 61).*

For Zarqa, too, what has to be done is not so complicated.

> *"... distinct and meaningful economics is not only possible but also necessary.... if we replace non-Islamic values by Islamic ones, and add to the economists' stock of positive assertions, Islamic assertions, we will be able to work out a meaningful distinct science of Islamic economics." (Khan; in Ahmed; 2002; 61).*

With regard to developments in macro-economics, Chapra says:

> *"Some progress has undoubtedly been made in macroeconomics. There has been a substantial discussion of the maqasid. There is, however, no theoretical model which would show how these goals may be realized. The attempts made so far "simply replace interest rate by profit-sharing ratio and introduce zakat as a tax without assuming any substantial change in the behaviour of the economic agents." (Chapra; 2001-a; 48).*

On macroeconomics, Tahir says:

> *"There is no existing Islamic economy, so to say, which can provide a basis for theorizing. However, this does not render Islamic macroeconomics an unnecessary exercise. On the contrary, it opens exiting possibilities for both theorists and policy-makers. It is our earnest belief that every action is <u>either</u> Islamic or Islamic. This simple observation provides both the rationale for the Islamic approach and its broad features in all disciplines in social sciences and humanities, including macroeconomics." (Tahir; in Kahf (Ed); 1998; 301).*

What about the micro-economics? Again, Chapra has something to say:

> *"The field where very little progress has been made is microeconomics.... Islamic economics has thus to establish the relationship between its macroeconomic goals and the behaviour of different economic agents through the development of a more realistic microeconomics. This may take place if there is "a separate theory of consumer behaviour and a separate theory of firm in the context of Islamic economics". Since no rigorous attempt has been made to fill this gap, Yalcintas is perhaps right in pointing out that: "Construction of microeconomic theory under the Islamic constraints might be the most challenging task before Islamic economics." (Chapra; 2001-a; 49).*

Expressing his discontent clearly with the condition of Islamic economics, Chapra continues:

> *"Islamic economics thus has a long way to go before it may be able to become a distinct economic discipline. It has so far scratched only the surface. Its theoretical core has, as*

---

3 Fiqh: Islamic jurisprudence.

4 Usool fiqh: Procedure of Islamic Jurisprudence.

rightly indicated by Seyyed Vali Reza Nasr, "failed to escape the centripetal pull of western economic thought, and has in many regards been caught in the intellectual web of the very system it set out to replace." (Chapra; 2001-a; 51).

Apparently, the shortcomings of Islamic economics are serious and those who deal with them should attempt to make more contributions in the fields of micro- and macro-economics. But, again according to Chapra: "**Islamic economics however has the advantage of benefiting from the tools of analysis developed by conventional economics**." (Chapra; 2001-a; 50).

Chapra should be aware of the lack of credibility ascribed to neoclassical "mainstream economics", nowadays. Dissatisfaction of with neoclassical teachings is constantly increasing, due to its theoretical shortcomings and its inadequacy in explaining "real" economic relationships (in Gürak; 2007). Economists recognize that alternative theories have been increasing both quantitatively and qualitatively. Thus, it would be disadvantageous for Islamic economists seek guidance from such an 'unhealthy' model.

T. Kuran is another well-known Islamic economist. After having questioned the difference between Islamic economics and the Western style of secular economics, T. Kuran poses a critical question: **Do we have a consistent and comprehensive pool of economic knowledge at hand**? T. Kuran attempts to answer this question, first by discussing the concept of Islamic economics.

"Islamic economics did not emerge from a drive to correct economic imbalances, injustices, or inequalities. The Indian Muslims who launched it in the 1940s were motivated by a desire to defend Islamic civilization against foreign cultural influences. For Sayyid Abul A'la Maududi, the Pakistani ideologist whose voluminous writings popularized the term "Islamic economics" and set the tone for later contributions to the literature, this new approach to economics was to be a vehicle for establishing, or reestablishing, Islamic authority in a domain where Muslims were falling increasingly under the influence of Western ideas. By replacing Western economic approaches with an Islamic one, he hoped to restore the Islamic community's self-respect and improve its cohesion.

Because Islamic economics was developed to serve cultural and political ends, it did not have to meet scientific standards of coherence, precision, or realism. It needed only to differentiate itself from the intellectual traditions that it was aiming to displace. Accordingly, contributions to Islamic economics typically begin by identifying the distinguishing characteristics of an Islamic economy. From Maududi to the present, the most fundamental of these characteristics has been the prohibition of interest. Two others have been zakait/(Zakat) **for foreign readers put this in brackets so they know it has already been stated***)/, which is an ancient redistribution system, and the requirement that economic decisions pass through an Islamic moral filter." (T.Kuran; 1995; 156).*

F. Kahn who says: "**... we need to develop Islamic Theory of Economics rather than Islamic Economic Theory**" asks 'why could we not reach where we wanted to be' and gives the reasons as stated below.

- *"Lack of vision about destination.*
- *Lack of vision about methodology.*
- *Lack of awareness of developments taking place around with respect to theory and practice in the area of economic activities.*
- *Absence of support (for research).*
- *Absence of lifetime commitment to produce an original scientific work in Islamic economics.*
- *Lack of holistic approach." (Khan; 2013; 97).*

Economists should always bear in mind that Islamic economics cannot be studied without taking into consideration the Islamic values and principles as declared in the Holy Koran. Kahf warns those who wish to establish an Islamic economic system:

> *"Driven by a sense of idealism, some of us attribute a special status to the general objectives of the Islamic economic system: Full employment, satisfaction of basic human needs, economic-cum distributive justice, development or improvement in the quality of economic life, economic power, etc." (Kahf; 2013-a).*

However, says Kahf:

> *"... a closer examination of these objectives indicates us that they are the same for each and all economic systems as usually expressed in their econo-political rhetoric throughout the human history. More specifically, these objectives are also the core objectives of socialism, communism and capitalism even anarchism and all or "isms." (Kahf; 2013-a).*

Some Islamic countries try to practice the values and principles of Islamic economics. But, according to T. Kuran, there seems to be only one sector which stands out; "Islamic banking" or the "Islamic finance system". We won't discuss this at this time. A quote from A. Rahman will suffice:

> *"Generally, when Islamic economists discuss the traditional categories of economics such as income, consumption, government expenditure, investment, and savings, they do so in terms of ethical statements and prescriptions and not in terms of analysis and empirical theory." (Rahman; in Hassan; 2013; 57).*

If we leave aside the contentious issues of interest rate and Zakat, the tax levied on the wealth of Muslims, there does not seem to be any significant difference in practice in regard to the role of a modern state, whether Islamic or Western.

Based on the opinions of the aforementioned Islamic economists we may conclude that Islamic economics has not yet reached the stage of having any alternative 'scientific' economic theory that significantly differs from the Western ones. In addition, we can confidently say that 'Homo Islamicus' still remains to emerge; except for some exceptional individual cases, of course. As T. Koran states; "**Islamic economics does not offer a comprehensive framework for a modern economy**." (T. Kuran; 1995; 170), yet.

However, as we know, there is no limit to human creativity. Alternative 'scientific' Islamic economic theories may emerge in time; a probability that should not be overlooked or underestimated.

A new Islamic economic paradigm with its new and alternative scientific Islamic economic theories will have to be so '**comprehensive**' as well as so '**perfect**' in regard to '**fairness**', '**ethical values**' and '**fruitfulness**', that when you take out the word "Islamic", it should appeal to all irrespective of gender, race or creed.

The Verses of the Koran & the Hadith[5] about "Alternative" Economics

So far, we haven't come across any Islamic 'scientific' economic theories in the 'scientific' works of Islamic economists. Is it possible to find these theories in the Holy Koran? On this matter, S.M.H. Zaman says:

> "... *the* Shari'ah *provides only some basic principles which guide economic behaviour of the individual and which point out to socially desirable objectives. This enables ample freedom within the specified limits to choose a strategy of action is not designed to lead to neglect of the basic objectives which are so essential in an Islamic society. These objectives are to discharge man's obligations to Allah which include those social responsibilities which Allah Himself has ordained. Thus a possible definition of Islamic economics incorporating these characteristics may be proposed as follows:*
>
> *Islamic economics is the knowledge and application of injunctions and rules of the Shari'ah that prevent injustice in the acquisition and disposal of material resources in order to provide satisfaction to human beings and enable them to perform their obligations to Allah and the society." (S.M.H. Zaman, 1984, 49-50)*

Briefly, according to S.M.H. Zaman: "**Islamic economics is the knowledge and application of injunctions and rules of the Shari'ah...**" The message is clear; if any alternative Islamic economic theories are to be constructed, economists

---

5 Hadith: a saying of the Prophet Muhammad.

should search for their keystones in the Holy Koran. After all, the primary purpose of all economic relationships or transactions, according to the Islamic faith and the Shariah is believed to be to secure the '**Falah**', ('**welfare**' in economic terms). The primary sources of the '**Falah**', according **to** M.E. Han are:

1. *"Koran.*
2. *Sunnah.*
3. *Fiqh.*
4. *History of Islam.*
5. *Facts of life." (Han; 1988; 34)*

M.A. Mannan points out four primary sources in order to reach the target of constituting an Islamic economic society:

1. *"Koran.*
2. *Hadith and Sunnah.*
3. *Ijma*[6].
4. *Ijtihad*[7]*." (Mannan; 29)*

According to Khan, Islamic law, Sharia, and matters of economic nature should not be considered separately. Because, he thinks: "**Roots of Islamic economics should, by definition, lie in *Fiqh*.**" (Khan; in Ahmed; 2002; 62). H. Ahmed presents a similar view:

> *"The underlying paradigm of the Islamic economic system is* Sharia'h. *The behavior of an 'Islamic man' based on* Shariah's *forms the micro-foundations of the Islamic economy (Ariff, 1985)". (Ahmed; in Ahmed; 2002; 124).*

All the opinions quoted above show us clearly that according to Islamic economists, each economic practice or transaction should be in compliance with the Islamic faith. However, this does not constitute any 'scientific' economic theory or economic model or method.

On the Koranic verses addressing economic transactions, S. Orman states that:

> *"We know that there are many Koranic verses which refer to economic transactions, directly or indirectly, explicitly or implicitly, particularly or in passing. If considered as pioneering and subjected to systematic and disciplined reasoning, one can establish a noteworthy consistency among them, as well as with some other Koranic verses, which constitutes an economic background and infrastructure.*
>
> *The Koran, with its peculiar method and procedure, refers to various economic issues, among others, to interest rate, Zakat, taxes, property, inheritance, economic motivation,*

---

6 Ijma: the consensus of 'all' Islamic judges on the rightness of a belief or practice.
7 Ijtihad: The process of arriving at new rules from recognized sources of Shariah.

interest free loans, subsistence, trade, measuring and weighing, opulence and poverty, economic contracts, particular work ethics and economic ethics in general." (Orman; 2010; 161-162).

S. Orman is correct in saying that some Koranic verses refer to all the economic fields and transactions that he mentioned. After all, the Koran is a holy book. It was meant to guide every aspect of the lives of Muslims with its detailed instructions, laws and principles. However, it is not our purpose to find references in the Koran concerning economic practices or transactions, but to find alternative 'scientific' economic theories applicable to all countries around the world, whether Muslim or non-Muslim. To be more specific, we are primarily interested in theories about value-price, growth, exchange, employment, etc. As S. Orman mentioned: **There is no need to say that the Koran is not an economics textbook** (Orman; 2010; 264).

It is imperative to show the utmost courtesy when using the word 'Islam' or 'the Koran' when referring to economic practices or transactions. Otherwise it may lead to a misunderstanding of the words used which may, in turn, result in undesired or unexpected consequences.

Ghazali, who had a distinguished place among Islamic scholars and economists, about 1000 years ago, expressed an interesting remark on gold and silver, claiming that:

"God appointed them as judges for the ascertainment of values and prices of all things and for their exchange" (Ashker-Wilson; 2006; 248).

Ghazali continued his remarks as follows:

"... the person who hoards gold and silver does oppress and makes inoperative the purpose for which God had made them". They are not meant to be for individuals per se but for being as a medium of exchange of goods." (Ashker-Wilson; 2006; 249).

And, Ghazali came to the conclusion that a person who is:

"... affecting the supply of these precious metals by using them for utensils, cups and the like, is sinful and the person in this case, **'acts contrary to the object for which these are created", and, "is ungrateful to God and commits sins.**" *(Ashker-Wilson; 2006; 249).*

Gazali is a highly intellectual and creative Islamic scholar, who even today, has a distinguished place amongst the Islamic jurists. How likely is it that an Islamic scholar of Gazali's caliber could be mistaken? Is it possible that Gazali, the most influential Islamic scholar of the time, could have misunderstood or misinterpreted the economic messages? In Ghazali's time gold and silver were the principle mediums of exchange. But, they are very rarely used as a medium in exchange today. If they were they indeed "**appointed by God**" as mediums of exchange, are we committing a sin by using "paper money" or some other "derivatives of money"? Today the main international mediums of exchange are the US dollar and the Euro created by their respective monetary authorities. Does this mean that Ghazali's conclusions are not valid in today's world?

If one truly believes that gold and silver were created by God merely as a medium of exchange, there is nothing left to say. For a faithful Muslim, God's will is the end of any discussion. If anyone dares to challenge God's will or instructions, he/she would be committing blasphemy and no good Muslim wants to be in that position. But, what if Ghazali was wrong? Should we accept Ghazali's interpretation as an "Islamic judgment" or "Islamic ruling"? Or simply as an interpretation of a philosopher called Ghazali? If someone opposes Ghazali's interpretation, would he/she be opposing Ghazali's 'interpretation' on the medium of exchange or opposing an "Islamic judgment" or ruling"?

Another Islamic economist commented on money. Neccar, who is considered to be one of the founders, if not 'The' founder, of the "interest rate free Islamic banking system" claims that whoever saves money (i.e., refrains from spending) commits a grievous sin. That is because; he/she would be refraining from spending a bounty provided by God, using it neither for personal use nor for the benefit of others (see Neccar, 1978, 211). Thus, according to Neccar, there seems to be some 'divine' rules about money. If there are indeed 'divine' rules, then nobody would dare to say anything against these rules because 'divine' rules are not subject to debate. But, what if there are no 'divine' rules or 'divine' principles in regard to savings. What if Neccar is misinterpreting the 'divine' expressions, and thus misguiding us?

M.A. Annan is another Islamic economist using the word 'Islam' in conjunction with economic concepts. According to Annan, the recognition of "the land" and "the laborer" as the two basic factors of production is a "unique" Islamic principle (M.A. Annan, 130). As far as we know, the Koran does not contain a concept called the 'production factor'. Therefore, Annan's claim represents only his opinion; it is not a 'divine' Islamic concept. Objecting to his claim that the land and the laborers are the two basic factors in production should not be considered as an opposition to Islamic teachings or the Koran.

H.Y. Apaydın sends out a warning to those who use economic concepts recklessly in conjunction with the word 'Islam'.

> *"It would be better to speak as a follower of a conventional idea, instead of speaking on behalf of Islam and the Koran. ... A man or a group of people who do not follow a conventional idea or who have no methodology, but attribute an anticipated social project to Islam or to the Koran ... are bringing Islam and the Koran into the playing field and,*

in a way, using them as a medium for the imposition of his/her or their opinions. ... In the final analysis, in order to account for the lack of emergence of conventional ideas, it can easily be declared that the 'totalitarian Islamic' mindset and its simplistic approach known as the 'according to the Koran mindset', had a big influence." (Apaydın, 87; in Demir, Ed. 1999).

F. Khan is also critical of using economic concepts recklessly.

"There has been undue obsession about the role of Fiqh in developing economics. Economics is a study of particular aspect of human behavior. Fiqh may guide us only to the institutional framework within which an Islamic agent is supposed to behave. But Fiqh cannot give us the scientific basis to study and analyze human behavior." (Khan; 2013; 96).

At this stage, it seems appropriate to return to our main question: Are there any 'divine' scientific economic theories or 'divine' methods of analysis in the verses of the Koran or in the Hadith? Can we find any reference to alternative 'scientific' economic theories on price, or growth, or trade in the Koran or the Hadith?

As far as we know, at this moment in time, according to the information we have, the answer has to be a resounding: NO! This should not come as a surprise because the Koran is neither a scientific textbook nor are the practices of the Prophet Muhammad meant to be an Islamic economic system.

Concluding Remarks

The well-known Scottish philosopher, Adam Smith, is recognized by many economists as the founder of modern economics. Since then, economics has developed and expanded rapidly around the world. Nowadays, those who are interested in economics and want to be an expert economist have to undergo a long process of training which has to be supported by some practical experience. In spite of all attempts to further develop economic knowledge, economists have failed to introduce coherent economic theories on the fundamental issues on which they unanimously agree. Until recently, the major economic theories which dominated academic economics were predominantly partly neoclassical and partly Keynesian. But these theories were subject to severe criticism and even considered fallacious by some (see Gürak, 2007). Nowadays, many new and alternative schools of economic thought (the 'heterodox economics') are emerging and growing rapidly. They are searching for more realistic approaches, analyses and methods.

Undoubtedly, economic relations and transactions today, are extremely complex, multi-dimensional and more multi-product than they were 1,000 years ago, or 100 years ago or even 20 years ago. It is very important to understand this difference, so that Islamic economics can develop appropriate economic theories and methods of analysis in order to enhance its economic growth. Those Islamic scholars who do not have an appropriate knowledge base nor experience in economics matters, would better serve the interests of Islam and their fellow Muslims by not intervening in matters for which they are not trained and leave economic matters to those who are trained to deal with them.

One important thing that needs to be emphasized is: According to the Islamic faith, every aspect of life has to be in accordance with the Koran or a Sunnah of the Prophet Muhammad. In other words, genuine Muslims have to pursue a lifestyle that is ordained by the verses of the Holy Koran and the Hadith (the practices of the Prophet Muhammad). Such a lifestyle inevitably puts the Islamic jurists, into a powerful and influential position in the everyday life of Muslims. Accordingly, Islamic jurists, expect every Muslim to obey the decisions they make which everyone expects to be" in accordance" with Islamic law. Those who disregard or dare to challenge these rulings may find themselves in very deep waters, and may even face accusations of being an 'infidel'.

It is not an uncommon to encounter incidences where a scholar defending ideas which run contrary to the Fatwas of the Islamic jurists are severely criticized or accused of committing an intolerable sin. For example, Farabi known to the West as **Alpharabius** and Ibn Sina known as **Avicenna**, who were, undoubtedly, true believers in Islam and who also had made significant contributions to the pool of global scientific knowledge about 1,000 years ago, were criticized severely by the Imam Ghazali and his followers because of their "different" philosophical stand points. After having studied the opinions of Farabi (Alpharabius) and Ibn Sina (Avicenna), Ghazali considered his criticism using 20 separate headings and claimed that 17 of the topics studied contained a 'deviance' and three of them were 'blasphemy'. According to Boer, Ghazali perceived the teachings of both Farabi (Alpharabius) and İbn Sina (Avicenna) as '**hostile to Islam**'.

The great Islamic philosopher of Andalusia Ibn Rushd known as **Averroes** had severely criticized Ghazali's opinions and claimed that **Ghazali had no intention of being constructive, only the intention of destroying the ideas of Farabi and especially of Ibn Sina** (see Uludag, 2004, 42). Today many scholars of philosophy share the opinion that Ghazali was mistaken in his criticisms. But, nevertheless, for many centuries these philosophers did not get the recognition they deserved in Islamic countries. Their philosophical contributions were ignored and overlooked in the Islamic education system. Meanwhile, the opinions of both philosophers, Farabi (Alpharabius) and Ibn Sina (Avicenna), amongst others, paved the way for scientific development in the West. Farabi once was considered "**The Second Teacher**" (muallim-i sâni) after of the founder of philosophy, Aristotle, **The First Teacher**, whose writings laid down the cornerstone of a comprehensive system of philosophy. And Ibn Sina, the founder of Islamic philosophy was considered as "**The Great Master**" (Sheikh al-Rayees) and was the most influential scholar in the Islamic Golden Age. I wonder what the Islamic world would look like today if Islamic countries followed in the footsteps of these great Turkish philosophers.

Bearing in mind how Farabi's and Ibn Sina's contributions were treated, the road on treads to develop alternative Islamic economic theories is highly formidable and risky. There is always a high risk of being severely criticized or even being called an "infidel" if new ideas deviate from the traditional ones laid down by "some" past Islamic scholars.

However, what comforts us is the fact that **Islam always welcomes and promotes scientific works and praises scholars**.

Chapter-2

Revaluation of Islamic Economics-2
Western Scientific Economic Theories

Are They A Proper Source of Inspiration for Islamic Economics?

Some Opinions on Islamic Economics

Once again, we need to point out the role of Islamic values and principles in determining the outcome of economic relations. And, once again, we should remember that there are no Islamic 'scientific' economic models which could pave the way for non-Muslim economists to follow the so called 'superior' Islamic economic system. There are certainly some definite Islamic "thoughts" on economic matters such as its approach to interest rate, how to behave as a "good" Muslim consumer, or how much Zakat to pay. Yet, these "thoughts" seem to be more like opinions, comments or mere criticisms rather than an advancement of an 'economic theory'. In addition, and more importantly, with regard to these 'scientific' theories, Islamic economics still lacks key theories on value-price, growth, trade, income distribution, employment and inflation.

A Hadith, (a saying of the Prophet Muhammad) states that:

"The wage of an employee should be paid before the worker's sweat dries on his brow".

Yet, there is no Islamic wage theory.

Again, according to the Prophet Muhammad:

"Nine-tenths of the material or spiritual food blessed by God, originates from trade".

But, surprisingly, despite the Prophet Muhammad being an accomplished trader, **Islamic economics lacks an international trade theory**. (see Güler; 2012; 17).

The critical question is: What are the Islamic economists doing in order to deal with these important omissions? Where should the Islamic economists look for appropriate "alternative" theories? In the Holy Book of the Koran? In the Hadith? Or, since the Holy Koran is not an economics text book, should they use their God-given intellectual talents to develop "new" and "alternative" economic theories?

Our proposition is; God gave intellectual talents to humans. So humans should use them to develop "new" and "alternative" economic theories. These theories should certainly be respectful of, responsive to and in accordance with, Islamic principles.

The Concept of Islamic economics

We need to remind ourselves how the notion of "Islamic economics" came into being. Islam as a universal religion was revealed in the 7th Century. However, the term "Islamic economics" was first used by Muslims of the Sub-Continent in the 1940s.

According to Kahf:

> *"Anwar Quraishi (1948) was perhaps the first economist who attempted to discover an Islamic Theory based on the prohibition of 'Riba' (interest rate). Since then we started having publications and research on Islamic economics by three breeds of people: socio-political activists, Shariah scholars with little exposure to some kind of economics and Western trained economists with little or not so little exposure to Shariah scholarship. Sorting these writings and publications is very important to understand the development of Islamic Economics in the second half of the past century.*
>
> *The first category of writings is normally general, political oriented and condensed in the form of social and political slogans. The second category is loaded with Fiqh in both methodology and focus; with extremely few exceptions it is more of Fiqh al Mu'amalat than any economics. Lastly a considerable chunk of the writings in the third category is based on a precept of self-proclaimed distinctiveness." (Kahf; 2013-a; 1).*

There is a large volume of literature on Islamic economics which has come into existence since the 1940s. However, it would be unrealistic to claim that Islamic economics has yet reached the point of maturity.

The quotations below from various Islamic economists display what they think about Islamic economics. Most of them are statements, explanations and comments in relation to the Islamic faith "as a religion" rather than objective economic evaluations based on a human's intellectual capability. 'Scientific' Islamic economic theories are either non-existent or merely based on "wishful thinking". There may even be some alternative theories in their infancy, which up to now, we know nothing about.

The first Islamic economist to refer to is one of the pioneers of research into Islamic economics. He is the Pakistani S.M. Hasanuz Zaman. In a detailed study on the concept of Islamic economics published in 1984, Zaman states:

> *"One way of defining Islamic economics is to qualify the term modern economics with Islam, viz. Islamic economics is 'the study of economics in the light of Islamic principles', or 'bringing economics in consonance with the* Shari'ah'. *But this would imply that the definition of the science of economics has a universal acceptability which it does not.*
>
> *Another way of defining Islamic economics would be to accommodate the latest and the least criticized definition of economics and qualify it with Islam. For example, if we accept Robbins' definition of economics, we could define Islamic economics as 'a science which studies human behavior as a relationship between ends and scarce means which have alternative uses, in the light of the* Shari'ah'.
>
> *But, firstly, this definition would invite criticism that has been made of Robbins' definition, and secondly, it would also raise the problem of reconciliation of incompatible concepts. The qualifying word 'Islamic' imposes on us a set of a* priori *judgments, and whether or not we are capable of rationally justifying them, we have to assume them as*

correct. Interest is prohibited whether or not monetary savings are scarce. Zakat *is incumbent whether or not there are needy people deserving it. Man's choice to consume anything and to any extent is not absolutely free.*

Defining Islamic economics would call for the accommodation of some prerequisites which are characteristic of the Islamic way of life. The first of such prerequisites is that in Islam economic activity ought not to be governed by human desire and experience alone, it should be governed by the fundamental injunctions of the Shari'ah. *As a social science, Islamic economics is not independent of moral values. Its normative aspect is more pronounced than its positive aspect; in fact it is the normative aspect which is instrumental in analyzing existing economic phenomena and in deciding proper courses of action in consonance with the Islamic objectives. The* Shari'ah *has specified those objectives which an individual as well as a society should endeavour to achieve." (Zaman; 1984; 49-50).*

Another prominent name in the subject Islamic economics is Chapra who draws our attention to an important issue:

"Islamic economics is based on a paradigm which has socio-economic justice as its primary objective (Qur'an; 57:25). This objective takes its roots in the belief that human beings are the vicegerents of the One God, Who is the Creator of the Universe and everything in it.

Unlike the secularist market paradigm, human well-being is not considered to be dependent primarily on maximizing wealth and consumption; it requires a balanced satisfaction of both the material and the spiritual needs of the human personality. The spiritual need is not satisfied merely by offering prayers; it also requires the moulding of individual and social behavior in accordance with the Shariah *(Islamic teachings), which is designed to ensure the realization of the* maqasid al-Shariah, *the goals of the* Shariah.*" (Chapra; 2001-a; 25).*

Chapra quotes some definitions in his work (Chapra; 2001-a) from other Islamic economists in his footnote '32' on pages 33 and 34. For example, another well-known Islamic economist M.A. Mannan defines Islamic economics as follows:

"Islamic economics is a social science which studies the economic problems of a people imbued with the values of Islam." The definition of Khurshid Ahmad states: "Islamic economics is 'a systematic effort to try to understand the economic problem and man's behaviour, in relation to that problem from an Islamic perspective." According to M. Nejatullah Siddiqi's definition: "Islamic economics is "the Muslim thinkers' response to the economic challenges of their times. In this Endeavour they were aided by the Qur'an and the Sunnah[8] as well as by reason and experience." M. Akram Khan has a similar definition: "Islamic economics aims at the study of human falah {well-being} achieved by organizing the resources of the earth on the basis of cooperation and participation." And,

8 Sunnah: the sayings and/or the practice of Prophet Mohammed.

again, according to the quotation by Chapra, Syed Nawab Haider Naqvi's definition is as follows: "Islamic economics is the representative Muslim's behaviour in a typical Muslim society." (Chapra; 2001-a).

Another Islamic economist Yousri (2013) defines Islamic economics as:

"Islamic economics is the science that studies the best possible use of all available economic resources, bestowed by Allah, for the production of maximum possible output of **Halal** *goods and services that are needed for the community now and in future and the just distribution of this output within the framework of* **Shariah** *and its intents." (A. Yousri; 2013; 16).*

According to this definition:

"... available resources have to be used according to the commands of Allah and in the manner that pleases him." (Yousri; 2013; 16).

As we know, Allah (God) is believed to have created sufficient resources for all mankind; the only differences lie in His blessing of different individuals. The faithful believers of Islam should attempt to produce only those products which are 'Halal' (permissible) and avoid those which are 'Haram' (prohibited) by their faith."

Another important message is in relation to the distribution of these resources:

"... the just distribution of this output must be within the framework of Shariah and its intents." (Yousri; 2013; 17).

Yousri has one more definition of Islamic economics:

"Islamic economics is the science which searches in the best possible use of human productive capacities and all resources bestowed by Allah in the manner that would yield maximum possible ***Halal Earnings*** *at present and in future, distributing and spending these earnings within the framework of* ***Shariah****." (Yousri; 2013; 17).*

Another Islamic economist Suwailem's definition of Islamic economics is as follows:

"Islamic economics is the study of Islamic principles concerning economic behavior. It includes the economic explanation of such principles, as well as their implementation and policy implications.

A brief outline of these principles includes:

1. *Material interest shall be balanced with spiritual and social interests.*
2. *Time horizon is extended beyond this world to include the Hereafter.*
3. *Zakat or obligatory charity is an essential duty.*

4. *Riba or interest on loans is strictly prohibited.*
5. *Gambling and wagering, or gharar in general, is also prohibited." (Suwailem; 2008; 81).*

Though Suwailem refers to Islamic principles, these principles, he claims, should be common to all celestial religions.

"What is different in case of Islam is the supporting detailed regulations regarding trade, partnership, inheritance, etc., known as Shari'ah." (Suwailem; 2008; 81).

Regarding the Islamic economics Zarqa asks some important questions:

"If we accept the existence of Islamic economics, does this not lead us to reject or deny the existence of universal economic regularities which operate in all human societies? [...] If it is Islamic, does it mean that it belongs to Muslim societies only or only operates in Muslim societies? How can we describe economics as Islamic or non-Islamic? If we usually do not like to talk about Islamic physics or Islamic geology, in what sense are we permitted to talk about Islamic economics and to add the adjective 'Islamic' to a social science?" (Zarqa; in Kahf (Ed. Vol.1); 1998; 129).

According to Zarqa, Islamic economics can adopt some things from conventional economics. For example:

"Conventional economics has some value judgments: some of them conform to the Shari'ah and some of them are in opposition to Shari'ah. [...] Positive assertion in economics I can take from Christian, Muslim, Buddhist or any other descriptive statements. Statements over regularities." (Zarqa; in Kahf Ed. Vol.1; 1998; 140).

However, Zarqa believes that there is only one source to guide the societies:

"It is my conviction that the Islamic Shari'ah *gives us a clear indication that there are universal laws and social laws applicable to all societies. As Muslims we believe that there are regularities in all human societies and the existence and universality of these regularities are the basic logic behind Allah (*Subhanahu wa Ta'ala*) choosing one* Shari'ah *to guide mankind until the day of judgement." (Zarqa; in Kahf Ed. Vol.1; 1998; 129-130).*

Tahir says:

"Since the Western values mostly clash with Islam, an appropriate response is to replace the unIslamic values by the Islamic values and to rework existing macroeconomics. This is the currently dominant Islamization of Knowledge approach." (Tahir; in Kahf Ed. Vol.1; 1998; 303).

Ashker-Wilson points out the significance of "Islamic man" or as some may prefer to say "Homo Islamicus", in the functioning of Islamic economics. The "Islamic man" is the epicenter of all economic relations.

"No successful Islamic system, and in this regard an Islamic economic system generally, can be perceived without a Muslim man. The Islamic society with all its Islamic

ingredients and beliefs is a pre-requisite for the application of an Islamic economic system successfully. The Islamic economic system and the sound Islamic, not only Muslim, society are inseparable, and there is no guarantee that the former will be successful without the latter. This emphasizes the need to have a well structured Islamic society in order to have a thriving Islamic economic system." (Ashker-Wilson; 2006; 394).

The common message in these definitions is their conformity to Islamic values and principles. Islamic economics cannot be studied without reference to Islamic principles. But, this conformity to Islamic principles is not a barrier to developing "new" and "alternative" scientific economic theories by using God-given talents, abilities and experience. Islamic economists have to move from a precatory state ("wishful thinking") to the generation and development of new economic theories compatible with Islamic principles. This should be the primary goal of the "creatively-minded" Islamic economists[9], which includes, by definition, all Islamic scholars interested on economic issues and especially those who have an appropriate background knowledge and/or experience in contemporary economics.

How Does One Proceed?

Islamic economists have two options in developing "new" theories:

1. To develop an entirely "new" theory using original economic theories.
2. To adapt, adjust and further develop existing economic theories developed in the west, i.e. non-Muslim countries.

1- Attempts to develop entirely new and original economic theories would be both irrational and a waste of valuable human resources. This is because the nature of economic transactions is, in principle, more or less of the same all over the world. For example, there are consumers who want to maximize the utility they get from their product at the lowest possible price in the competitive markets, regardless of their religion, race or creed. On the other hand, there are producers who want to produce low cost products and to maximize their profits, regardless of their religion, race or creed. These basic behaviors do not change much in different countries. In addition, the role of the government and state organs is to set the rules of the game and to see that everybody conforms to these rules. Since the nature of global economic

9 From now on, the term Islamic economist includes all Islamic scholars interested on economic issues and endowed with appropriate background knowledge, skills and experience on contemporary economics.

relationships, its related problems and the potential remedies are similar; there is no need to "rediscover" available knowledge on the subject. What is available can be a good starting point in finding the "right" path.
2- Having said that: onto the second option i.e. to adapt, adjust and to further develop the already highly developed existing economic theories used by other non-Islamic economists. This seems a natural and rational choice.

But, having decided which approach one is going to take is not the end of the problem; merely the beginning!

Bearing in mind the irreversible and indispensable role of Islamic principles on economic thinking and in the formulation of any theory; which non-Islamic economic theories should be used as sources for Islamic economists? After all, the religious principles do matter and they play a determinant role in the economic transactions of "Homo Islamicus" who is a very different man from the "Homo Economicus" of the neoclassical model. As we know, there is no place for religious, historical, institutional or, in fact any other value in western economic models. Main stream ideology, e.g., the neoclassical model has, in fact, no place at all for historical, cultural, religious developments or for the differing institutions in other countries. If western theories are to be a source of inspiration or a starting point for Islamic economics, then Islamic economists have to be extremely careful in their choice of theories, before they begin.

Some Features of the Mainstream Theory

When anyone talks about economic theories the first ones that spring to mind are the Neoclassical, Marxist and Keynesian ones. There are also relatively new theories known as "Heterodox economics". But it wouldn't be unfair to say that these theories are still in the developmental stage. The most frequently and widely used economic theory is the neoclassical ones, e.g. the "mainstream theories". Every economics student becomes acquainted with the mainstream theories during their education in the west. It is more than likely that all Islamic economists have, in one way or another encountered these neoclassical theories during their economics education. Thus, the mainstream theories do, inevitably, represent an important potential source of inspiration for Islamic economists in their development of Islamic economics. As a matter of fact, for the economist Ahmed a solution is at hand and there's no need to search for it elsewhere.

> *"... even though the paradigm of an Islamic economic system is different from the neoclassical one, the basic principles of the marginalist analytical tools do not contradict Islamic*

principles and can be used to study the underlying behavior of agents in an Islamic system." (Ahmed; in H.Ahmed; 2002; 126).

Khan shares a similar view to Ahmed and proposes a simple solution:

"Islamic economics can be discussed under the neoclassical framework by simply adding Islamic values to it." (in H.Ahmed; 2002; 126).

Does Ahmed have a good and solid point? Do neoclassical theories indeed represent a proper and appropriate guide or inspiration for the further development of Islamic economics?

In principle, our response to these questions is; a very "qualified" "yes".

The Nature of the Neoclassical Theories

Neoclassical economics claims, just as the natural sciences do, to have "universally applicable" and "scientific" economic laws, free of subjective values, ethics, and all other non-scientific inputs. However, neoclassical theories have many serious shortcomings and many aspects of which are subject to severe criticism, not to mention their "non-religious" and "value-free" nature. The claim of "universality" alone is sufficient to label it "invalid". It cannot be validated globally, due to its shortcomings in regard to economic relationships in national economies. The assumptions are, predominantly, "utopian", unrealistic and seem to be applicable to "academic" models rather than to real ongoing economic relationships. These so-called "scientific" analyses often refer to abstract, mechanical and fictitious economic relationships, completely divorced from reality. There is no place for values, especially religious values. In addition, historical events and their influence on economic development are ignored, along with the influence of any institutional factor. These inadequacies clearly indicate the inability of the neoclassical models to cope with real economic issues. So as a starting point for the development of an Islamic economic theory, the neoclassical theories are poor and inadequate sources of inspiration. Furthermore it is also an inadequate source of economic knowledge as it does not conform to the actual events found in national or global economic relationships.

Do Assumptions have to be "Utopian"?

When one is constructing a theory, do the assumptions used in the theory always have to be academic or utopian in nature? Or, can they pertain to the facts and be realistic. If we look at the neoclassical models in the light of these two questions one can see that their theory of price has many unrealistic assumptions. For example, the neoclassical price theory assumes that, under fully competitive conditions, price is a "given", products are "homogenous", entry into the market is "free", e.g. unrestricted and there is a "perfect flow of information". If there is no intervention, the markets are assumed to automatically reach a state of "equilibrium".

Do these basic assumptions of the neoclassical price theory enable us to understand, to describe, to explain, to find remedies for problems that occur and to predict future events correctly? Or, are these assumptions in fact irrelevant, too abstract, or "utopian" and merely simplify the actual economic dynamics which actually cause us "not" to comprehend fully what is really going on the market.

In order to research or analyze or to produce theories that explain economic phenomena, the economist, like any other scientist, naturally does have to simplify, abstract and generalize. If this were not the case, given the countless variables and the constant changes occurring between economic transactions, a proper analysis could not be made nor could any theories be produced. For example, one could not possibly hope to collect all the information about each and every consumer's expected expenditure or their trends in expenditure, in a single country, within a reasonable time frame. Let's assume that an economist has an unlimited amount of time and resources and he completes his "mission impossible". By the time he actually finishes it, everything will be different due to the constant flux in the trends of economic transactions. Therefore, an economist is obliged to make use of some **simplifying and abstract assumptions**. However, these assumptions, on the other hand, have to be as realistic as possible and must also be liable to testing, replication or rejection. For example, the neoclassical assumption of price being a "given" is a "simplifying" assumption but it has no relevance to reality at all. So what is the use of making such a utopian assumption in a scientific analysis? This line of criticism also applies to the other assumptions mentioned earlier.

The neoclassical theories claim to be "positive scientific" theories. This means they claim to be as "scientific" as the "natural" sciences (physics, astronomy, chemistry etc.). But, the natural sciences do not make "utopian" assumptions. For example, in California when someone plans to build a new house, nobody would dare to say to the client; "Let's assume that there's no earthquakes in California, so we don't need to……"

Let us consider another "utopian" assumption. As far as we know potatoes do not grow on the surface of Mars. Now, imagine an economist who claims that: "Let's assume that potatoes grow on the surface of Mars" and starts calculating the annual income from the potato output on Mars. Who would take this economist seriously?

Making "simplifying" assumptions and "utopian" assumptions are two completely different things with two different outcomes. An economist has to be able to differentiate between the "simplifying" assumptions from the "fallacies". As the Nobel Laureate Solow once stated, important assumptions have to be "**reasonably realistic**". If the conclusion of a theory is based on a special assumption and this assumption is a fallacy, then the conclusions are bound to be dubious or fallacious[10] (Solow; 1956; 65).

Making simplifying assumptions and "utopian" assumptions are two completely different things with different outcomes. An economist has to be able to differentiate the simplifying assumptions from the "fallacies". As the Nobel Laureate Solow once stated; the important assumptions have to be "**reasonably realistic**". If the conclusion of a theory is based on a special assumption and this assumption is skeptical, then the conclusions are bound to be skeptical, too. (Solow; 1956; 65).

The Historical Dimension

One major defect in the neoclassical models is the lack of any historical perspective. There have been many serious incidences in the past that influenced economic, social and political developments. The impacts of these historical events have influenced and have caused many of today's economic conditions and the economic differences between countries. If a particular country is relatively less developed today, we have to look to the past for the underlying causes.

But, the neoclassical models are not interested in such vital historical ingredients. It doesn't take any historical context into account; it fails to explain it; maybe its protagonists are ashamed of what happened. Yet, today, we appear to want to know, in great detail, why some countries are poorer than others. Could this be, as some racists suggest, that they are mentally inferior to "us"? Could it be that their political and economic systems contribute to their lack of development? What past global economic influences could have caused this widening income (development) gap between countries? Could we actually say that, the

10 "A 'crucial' assumption is one on which the conclusions do depend sensitively, and it is important that crucial assumptions be reasonably realistic. When the results of a theory seem to flow specifically from a special crucial assumption, then if the assumption is dubious, the results are suspect." (Solow; 1956; 65).

people of Europe are intellectually superior and more creative than those in the less developed countries? If this were the case, then how can we account for the rapid industrialization of the "Asian late- comers" like Japan and South Korea? The neoclassical models have no explanation at all, for any of these questions. And this lack of explanation doesn't seem to bother the neoclassical economists, one iota.

A Fictitious Case: The State of Equilibrium

The concept of "**equilibrium**" or "**equilibrium analysis**" is another weak or "fallacious" link in the neoclassical models. As we all know, real economies are "dynamic". This is due to the continuous introduction of new products and the introduction of new production methods based on continuous technological change. The assumption of a "static equilibrium" model by a so called "scientific" economic theory is "illogical" and is contrary to the very nature of scientific methodology.

"Static equilibrium" can only be validated if we were to take a "snapshot" at a particular place and time. But this is only one moment in the continuum of time. Economic transactions are in a continuous state of flux. The question is; how valuable is this "instantaneous" data in comprehending actual dynamic economic relationships?

Economy has never been in equilibrium as the neoclassic model claims. How can there be a long term static equilibrium when new technology is continually being introduced and employed. There is only one case where "static equilibrium can occur; in the minds or the academic models of neoclassical economists. So, what is the purpose or practical use of such an "equilibrium analysis"?

Utility

The concept "**utility**" is one of the most frequently used "key concepts" of neoclassical economics. But, it is, at the same time, perhaps the most "unscientific" and controversial. That is because, "utility", which means the satisfaction gained from the products obtained, is a highly "**subjective**" and largely a "**non-measurable**", concept. And as such, there should be no place for it in the "scientific" neoclassical models.

Let us assume that neoclassical economists do use this concept and are fully aware of its "subjective" and "non-measurable" features. In that case, they should not have assigned such an influential role to it and should warn the readers that it is not a truly "scientific" concept that can be found in the methodology used by the natural sciences.

Previously economic theorists made optimistic attempts to measure utility by naming it "cardinal utility". However, they soon realized that this was a hopeless task. Later others made new attempts by using "indifference curves" defining them as the measurement of the "ordinal" utility. Despite their shortcomings, the "ordinal" utility concept and "indifference curves" are still a vital element of the neoclassical models. The question is; why did the neoclassical economists not completely abandon the concept? The answer is simple; if you take the "utility" concept out of the neoclassical models, there will be an abyss that needs to be filled.

Homo Economicus vs. Normal Man

Homo Economicus, the "utopian" economic man, created by the neoclassical economists is some kind of robot without feelings, emotions or a past. But, she/he behaves mechanically without any consideration for the well-being of other people, other nations or the environment. She/he is selfish, putting maximization of self-interest before all else. But she/he is also supposed to be rational!

Man in real-life has totally different characteristics from this neoclassical economic man. They both are described as rational. But, the real-life man is always influenced by the social, cultural and political events occurring around her/him. As a matter of fact, the real-life man sometimes behaves in a completely opposite manner to that which is expected from a Homo Economicus. For example, assume that there are two families; one, a Homo Economicus family and one a real-life family. Both of them are assumed to have saved 100,000 TL to buy the car they want so much. But, at the same time, both families have a sick child in need of an urgent operation that costs 100,000 TL, i.e. the exact amount saved for the purchase of car. What would the choice of each family be; buy the car or spend it on the operation for their child?

There is no need for the real-life family to evaluate their options. There can only be one option; the operation for the child. This is the natural and expected behavior from human beings with feelings and a responsibility to their child. But, this behavior would not be considered "rational" by the Homo Economicus family. The purchase of the car should be given the preference. Simply; the cost of making another child is practically zero. But, saving another 100,000 TL might take a very long time; and may never be realized in their life-time.

What a respectable scientific behavior!
Table:1 shows which assumptions of the mainstream model are "utopian", which are "realistic" and which are "normative". As we see, the first five assumptions are "utopian". But, they can be classified as "normative" as well.

Table:1 The major assumptions of the mainstream theories

	Utopian	Normative	Positive
Price is a "given"	X	X	-
Free Entry into the Market	X	X	-
Perfect information	X	X	-
Divisibility	X	X	-
Equilibrium	X	X	-
Homo Economicus	X	-	-
Law of Decreasing Returns	X	-	-
Productivity of Capital	X	-	-
Homogenous Product	X	-	-
S=I	X	-	-
Total Factor Productivity	X	-	-
No Transport Cost	X	-	-
No Intervention in Market	X	-	-

In short: mainstream economic models have many serious shortcomings which prevent us from fully comprehending what really happens in the markets, to find remedies or to make predictions. There are certainly some similarities to actual events, but they seem to be coincidences. When we consider the similarities, we can use the analogy of a broken watch which shows the time correctly twice a day. If you take a look at the watch at a specified time, you will see that it shows the time correctly. This is what the mainstream models offer us, with regard to real economic relationships.

What is the Attraction of the Neoclassical Theories?

In spite of a poor relevance to reality, fallacious assumptions and severe shortcomings, text books based on the neoclassical models continue to dominate the global academic environment. There is no other model that is accepted so widely, even including the Marxist and Keynesian models. The question is: **Is there any other social science that can deal with actual economic problems other than using a neoclassical model with its many "utopian" assumptions, its essential**

inadequacy in dealing with actual problems, and its spurious claims to a "scientific" basis?

The main reason that the neoclassical models, despite all their shortcomings, is still so widely acknowledged, is the "ideological support" it so generously receives from academics, publishers, and certain sections of the scientific world.

Another reason is the failure of academics to develop "alternative" logical, consistent and explanatory economic models. As Solow once confessed with regard to the scientific (!) mainstream models; "I know the wheel is crooked but it's the only game in town".

Well, maybe there are "other games in town" nowadays. But mainstream economists would be reluctant to use the "other wheel" due to the extensive efforts made on behalf of the existing theories. What would happen to all the effort made, the learned treatise written and the reputations earned so far? How would the past be accounted for? Would; "Sorry! It was all a big mistake", be sufficient?

A Brief Glance at the Past

In order to fully grasp the present situation, we have to make a little detour into the past and consider the prevailing conditions in the 19th Century and remember the radical movements that occurred especially between the 1850s and the 1870s.

The foundation stone of the neoclassical ideology, which at the time was known as the Marginalist School, was laid down in the 1870s in order to meet the radical challenge of the Marxism. The Marxist storm began approximately in the 1850s and threatened the capital-owners (the capitalists). They urgently had to find new weapons to fight the progress of Marxism and to preserve the then system. At that time; the working and living conditions of the labor force was so desperate, their social and political rights so restricted and future expectations so limited, that they had nothing left to lose but "their chains".

But, how did this situation arise?

The generally acknowledged founder of modern economics, the philosopher A. Smith had developed a new economic theory in order to display the superiority of the capitalist economic order over the Mercantilist economic order and ideology. Smith's theories were further developed by, among others, Ricardo, a rich businessman. However, while trying to develop new theories, economists had inevitably and unwittingly laid the corner stone for a new theory that would shake the foundations of the new economic order they wanted to build. This new theory was the Marxist theory of "class struggle and the exploitation of the laborer".

The Marxist theories were, to large extent, based on concepts developed by A. Smith and Ricardo such as, labor-force, surplus, labor-time, etc. It was not easy at all for the apologist of capitalism to account satisfactorily as to why the capitalist class owned the entire product produced by the "labor-power". The question of exploitation was asked openly and loudly and there was a weak response. In the meantime, the capitalists were getting richer, causing the functional and household income gap between the capitalists and the laborers to widen continuously. If the labor of the working class was the origin of all wealth created, the status quo could not be accepted. Revolution was looming large.

Under the circumstances, three economists came to rescue. In the 1870s Jevons, Menger and Walras started developing alternative theories later called the "Marginalist School". Their primary purpose was to present new and "scientific" (!) theories based on a form of "pure economics", free from subjective values. Thus, the focus of their work had to change from "political economics" to simply "economics". One of their main objectives was to prove that the laborer was not the only "productive" factor of production; that capital is also a "productive" factor.

One of the objectives of the creators of this "pure" economics was to prove that economics is a science, exactly like the natural sciences, with its own universally applicable valid laws. Everything could be measured, so they believed in this new "economic science". To prove their point, they developed mathematically sophisticated models functioning in accordance with "universally valid" laws. The source of inspiration was Newtonian mechanics. New economic theories have been developed since then, and finally, the neoclassical economists have developed highly sophisticated models of which they can be proud. But, can they also be proud of the "irrelevance" or "shortcomings" of their sophisticated theories?

By the way, the Natural Sciences which inspired economists have changed radically. But the scientific economists (!) have preferred to remain loyal to the original laws of Newtonian Mechanics. This resulted in what the Nobel Laureate Ronald Coase called "**blackboard economics**". Or, as another Nobel laureate John Hicks pointed out: "**The neoclassical economists have, with great skill, managed to pull a rabbit out of the hat**". But they can't explain how the rabbit got there.

A long time has passed since the 1870s and the Marxist storm has lost quite a lot of its original impact. In fact, nowadays it has turned into something of a nostalgic soft wind. It seems like the right time to reconsider the impact of the Marxist theories and revaluate or restructure other scientific (!) economic theories, including Keynes' contribution. And the point of departure in developing new and more realistic economic theories should be a new value-price theory; which is the corner stone of all other economic theories.

"Normative" Neoclassical Theories

In terms of "purely academic" standards, one has no choice but to admit that the neoclassical scholars have been quite successful in developing sophisticated alternative models and methods of analysis to counter the Marxist challenge. In other words, they have managed to "**pull a rabbit out of the hat**". Despite that amazing feat, the neoclassical theories cannot escape the criticism of being sterile, utopian and unrealistic. Sometimes the neoclassical scholars were even criticized for putting too much effort into "fallacies". But, can the critics claim that the neoclassical models are totally useless?

Well one answer is; it depends on how you look at them. As a matter of fact, the neoclassical theories and their models can make quite a significant contribution to the science of economics if they are revaluated from a different angle. The only thing to do is to acknowledge that the neoclassical theories and models are a "**normative**", instead of a "positive" science.

Positive Economics vs. Normative Economics

What is the difference between "positive" and "normative" economics?

"**Positive economics**" refers to a social science that deals primarily with the answers to questions starting with "why **is**?", or "what **is** it?" or "how **does** it work?" The method is one of "empirical" observation, evaluation of the collected data and the measurement of economic magnitudes or extent. It aims to explain present conditions, find remedies to occurring problems and to predict future conditions, irrespective of any subjective values or ethics. It is sometimes known as "value-free economics". Economic relationships and transactions are based on "independent economic laws" like those in the "natural sciences". And, of course, the neoclassical models are a perfect example of this.

"**Normative economics**" deals with a form of economics unencumbered by "subjective values". The questions normally start with "what **should** it be, how **should** it be?" and reflects certain prescribed values and premises. The prescriptive nature of these questions often provokes serious debate among economic scholars. Usually their prescriptions are related to future developments or changes. For example; "How **income should** be redistributed?" or "How production relationships **should** be shaped?" are some typical "normative" questions.

Neoclassical models have the potential to make a significant contribution to economics as long as they are used as "**normative**" models. The reason for this is that their aim is to produce a "**better**" economic system. For example, having "perfectly competitive" conditions would be highly desirable from the consumers' points of view who obviously want to maximize their utility given their income. Since we do not have an economic system where "perfectly competitive" conditions apply, we should therefor do our best to create such a society.

Using one of the other norms; everyone knows that a "perfect flow of information" does not happen in the real world. However, it is highly desirable to have a free and unconditional access to information. If this actually happened, it would contribute significantly to a more efficient supply of products and to a more enlightened behavior with regard to product consumption. So we can, in reality, benefit from the neoclassical "normative" models to "better" our society. We know that we are speaking to the converted, but "better" is a subjectively value-loaded term.

On scientific (!) mainstream economics

Some economists may feel upset by these criticisms and say that the neoclassical theories do not deserve such scathing remarks. As the matter of fact, these criticisms are not restricted to the ranks of the opponents of the neoclassical theories. Below are some "negative" comments from some prominent neoclassical economists. None are Marxist or radical leftist economists. Here are their views without comment.

After having criticized Walras' "general equilibrium" analysis, the well-known economic historian Blaug continues:

> *"Here is a theory with absolutely no empirical content. Having "proved" the existence, uniqueness and local stability of multi-market general equilibrium, what have we learned about the economy? Absolutely nothing." (Blaug;in Skousen; 2001; 217).*

And some other related comments/views:

> *"Tremendous ingenuity has been applied over several decades to the task of adapting general equilibrium theory to the needs of macroeconomic theory. This effort, I believe, must by now be judged a failure." (A.Leijonhufvud: in Zambelli, 2010; 68).*

> *"A person is not likely to be a good economist who is nothing else." (J.S. Mill; in Marshall, 1990; 636).*

> *"... economics cannot be compared with the exact physical sciences: for it deals with the ever changing and subtle forces of human nature." (Marshall; 1990; 12).*

"The laws of economics are to be compared with the laws of the tides, rather than with the simple and exact law of gravitation. For the actions of men are so various and uncertain..." (Marshall; 1990; 26).

"The part played by the net product at the margin of production...is apt to be misunderstood. In particular many able writers have supposed that it represents the marginal use of a thing as governing the value of the whole. It is not so; the doctrine says we must go to the margin to study the action of those forces which govern the value of the whole: and that is a very different affair." (Marshall; 1990; 339-340).

"Later in life, Marshall was to regret this attempt to scientize economics, suggesting that we are still greatly ignorant of economic behavior..." (Schumpeter; in Skousen; 2001; 194).

"... economic science is a system of a priori truths, a product of pure reason, an exact science reaching laws as universal as those of mathematics, a purely axiomatic discipline, a system of pure deductions from a series of postulates, not open to any verification or regulation on the grounds of experience." (Machlup; in Caldwell; 1994; 140).

"...the postulates of the classical theory are applicable to a special case only and not to a general case...... its teaching is misleading and disastrous if we attempt to apply it to the facts of experience." (Keynes; 1973; 3).

"The fact that our knowledge of the future is fluctuating, vague and uncertain, renders wealth a peculiarly unsuitable subject for the methods of classical economic theory. ... There is no scientific basis on which to form any calculable probability whatsoever. We simply do not know." (Keynes; in Skousen,2001; 339).

"... human decisions affecting the future ... cannot depend on strict mathematical expectation, since the basis for making such calculations does not exist." (Keynes; 1991; 162-163).

"The neoclassical heritage still has a great influence, not only on the teaching of economics but in forming public opinion generally or at least in providing public opinion with its slogans. But when it comes to an actual issue, it has nothing concrete to say." (Robinson; 1962).

"Economics is a social study. It is concerned with the operations of human beings, who are not omniscient, and not wholly rational; who (perhaps because they are not wholly rational) have diverse, and not wholly consistent, ends. As such, it cannot be reduced to a pure technics." (Hicks; 1983; 289).

By the way, according to one prominent economist, Harrod:

"Keynes had no revolutionary contribution which substantially affected economic theory. *The main contribution of Keynes was the influence he had in readjusting the traditional theory and then the pertinent issues" (Harrod; 1937; 85).*

Now let's have a look at some recent criticisms and see what Hicks, Friedman, Leontief, Samuelson, et al., have to say:

"Pure economics has a remarkable way of producing rabbits out of hats -apparently a priori propositions which apparently refer to reality. It is fascinating to try to discover how they got in; for those of us who do not believe in magic must be convinced that they got in somehow." (Hicks; 1983; 367).

"People, not mechanical "laws of the market," should be the focus of the discipline." (R.T. Ely, founder of AEA; in Skousen; 2001; 235).

"... economics has become increasingly an arcane branch of mathematics rather than dealing with real economic problems." (Friedman; 1953).

"Page after page of professional economic journals are filled with mathematical formulas [...] Year after year economic theorists continue to produce scores of mathematical models and to explore in great detail their formal properties; and the econometricians fit algebraic functions of all possible shapes to essentially the same sets of data." (Leontief; http-4).

"Gunnar Myrdal, the Swedish economist, was able to convince the (Swedish) academy that economics, more than any other social science, had achieved such a high level of scientific inquiry that it deserved special honors (Nobel Prize) (although he later recanted and wished he had refused the prize because, he now argued, economics could not match the precision and value of the physical sciences)." (Skousen; 2001; 394).

"There is really nothing more pathetic than to have an economist or a retired engineer try to force analogies between the concepts of physics and the concepts of economics." (Samuelson, Nobel Prize Lecture, 1970).

"... nothing is impossible in an inexact science like economics." (Samuelson; 1973; 5).

"It has sometimes been suggested that our most advanced students know everything except common sense." (Samuelson, in Skousen; 2001; 94).

"Samuelson's book is practically nothing but differential equations and assumptions far removed from reality." (Skousen; 2001; 93).

"... the theory effectively denies the continuing and self-sustaining process of expansion of capital as an essential feature of the capitalist mode of production." (Harris; 1978; 20).

Solow once confessed:

"I know the wheel is crooked, but it's the only game in town" (Solow; in Skousen; 2001; 214).

Solow has more to say:

"A 'crucial' assumption is one on which the conclusions do depend sensitively, and it is important that crucial assumptions be reasonably realistic. When the results of a theory seem to flow specifically from a special crucial assumption, then if the assumption is dubious, the results are suspect." (Solow; 1956; 65).

"The markets for goods and for labor look to me like imperfect pieces of social machinery with important institutional peculiarities." (Solow; Dec. 1987).

" ... factor proportions might be variable only at the instant of gross investment and not after capital equipment had taken some particular form." (Solow; Dec. 1987).

"Today if you ask a mainstream economist a question about almost any aspect of economic life, the response will be: suppose we model that situation and see what happens... modern mainstream economics consists of little else but examples of this process." (Solow; http-4).

Additional confessions by Morishima, J.Stiglitz and R.Coase:

"Mathematical economic theory has recently become more and more abstract, transparent and sterile." (Morishima; in Skousen; 2001; 359).

"The models were fundamentally wrong in that they assumed perfect information, perfect competition, and no technical change... Anybody looking at these models would say they can't provide a good description of the modern world." (Stiglitz; in Cassidy; 1996; 56)

"As questionable as those might be for an advanced industrial economy, they are clearly not appropriate for developing countries." (Stiglitz; 1999; 11).

"[Economics as taught] in America's graduate schools... bears testimony to a triumph of ideology over science." (Stiglitz; http-4).

"What is studied is a system which lives in the minds of economists but not on earth. I have called it 'blackboard economics'." (Coase; Dec. 1991).

"Existing economics is a theoretical [meaning mathematical] system which floats in the air and which bears little relation to what happens in the real world." (Coase; http-4).

According to Lucas, "mechanics of development" refers to:

"... the construction of a mechanical, artificial world, populated by interacting robots that economics typically studies." (Lucas; 1988; 5).

"Economics is a primitive science, and there is a lot we don't know." (Lucas; in Cassidy; 1996; 52)

"I write down a bunch of equations, and I say this equation has to do with people's preferences and this equation is a description of the technology... But that doesn't make it so." (Lucas; in Cassidy; 1996; 55).

P. Romer, D. North and Blaug think:

"One of the overriding problems of economics is that it is non-experimental science." (Romer; 1994).

"We live in an uncertain and ever-changing world that is continually evolving in new and novel ways. Standard theories are of little help in this context. Attempting to understand

economic, political and social change requires a fundamental recasting of the way we think." (North; http-4).

"Modern economics is sick. Economics has increasingly become an intellectual game played for its own sake and not for its practical consequences for understanding the economic world. Economists have converted the subject into a sort of social mathematics in which analytical rigour is everything and practical relevance is nothing." (Blaug; in Hodgson; 2004).

Now let us examine some recent criticisms, for instance those of the Head of The Association of National Business Economists and a senior economist of A.T & T, Mark Dadd:

"Academic economics has taken a very bad turn in the road... It is very academic, very mathematical...it is nothing like as useful to the business community as it could be." (Cassidy; 1996; 51)

According to Cassidy, some firms are closing down economics departments and will benefit from this action.

"In recent years... some of the biggest companies in the country, including I.B.M., General Electric, and Kodak, have closed down their economics department. Meanwhile, many of the fastest-growing businesses in the economy... –have managed to prosper with the aid of hardly any economists at all." (Cassidy; 1996).

And finally what Roche has to say about economic education is highly likely to upset traditional neoclassical economists.

"We insist on at least three-to-four-year cleansing experience to neutralize the brainwashing that takes place in these graduate programs." (Cassidy; 1996; 51-52).

A final word of caution for Islamic economists who intend to benefit from the neoclassical models to develop Islamic economics using alternative theories: "**It is essential to know the direction of the wind, if you want to arrive at the planned destination safely with your boat.**"

However, in order to reach the targeted destination, the direction of the neoclassical winds does not seem blow in the appropriate direction.

Chapter-3

Revaluation of Islamic Economics-3
Islam, Science and the "Absolute Truth"

Introduction

Our purpose in this section is to study the differences between "scientific truth" and religious truth". Specifically, man carries out "scientific" research in order to understand and explain what occurs in Nature or to find out the cause-effect of economic relationships. Any religion, on the other hand, requires the unconditional acceptance of Divine truths revealed through their prophets. Our intention is to discuss this different perception in relation to the non-Islamic economic approach and Islamic economic theories.

The Positive Sciences – Economics & "Absolute Truth"

Human beings have always been curious about their environment and have been looking for ways to explain what causes certain natural occurrences. Even if we accept that neither human curiosity nor ingenuity has any bounds, there are still countless questions that need answering. As long as man continues to exist and has a functioning brain, further questions are bound to occur and answers need to be found. Humans began with "simple" questions; how to feed, clothe and protect themselves. As civilization progressed, the questions, and their answers, became more complex. Whether these questions concerned natural occurrences or social events, the purpose of human beings switched from attempts to understand their environment, to those questions that were concerned with changing the environment in which they lived. Questions and theories about future developments began to be the subject of their intellectual endeavors.

In the natural sciences, questions such as: What causes earthquakes? What would the expected amount of damage be after an earthquake? What sort of construction material should we use in building houses to minimize the extent of this damage? When and where will next earthquake occur? are some of the most frequently asked questions.

In the field of economics, some of the frequently asked questions are: What determines the value or price of a product? Do the supply and demand conditions have an impact on the market price? If so, then how? To what extent? How do we cope with the economic cycles? What is the cause of inflation?

The essential reason for asking these questions in the areas cited above is to ascertain whether there are any "**absolute truths or absolute facts**" that we can use. If the answer is 'yes', then do we know what they are?

We will attempt to answer these questions by separating "science" into two major groups:

1. Natural sciences such as physics, astronomy, biology.
2. Social sciences such as economics, politics, sociology.

"Natural" Sciences and the "Absolute Truth"

Sciences such as physics, astronomy, biology, chemistry are called the "Natural Sciences" which seek to elucidate the laws that govern the natural world. The cornerstone of the scientific method is "quantitative analysis".

> *"The subject of natural science consists of the various forms of the motion of matter in nature: their material bearers (substratum), forming a scale of successive levels in the structural organization of matter; their interrelationships, inner structure, and genesis; the basic forms of all existence—space and time; and the regular link between natural phenomena both general (embracing a number of forms of motion) and specific (relating only to individual aspects of various forms of motion, their substratum and structure).*
>
> *The goals of natural science are twofold: (1) to discover the essence of natural phenomena and their laws and, on this basis, to foresee or to create new phenomena; and (2) to reveal the potential for utilizing in practice the known laws, forces, and substances of nature. It may be said that the cognition of truth (that is, of the laws of nature) is the direct or most immediate goal of natural science and that facilitating the practical use of such laws is the ultimate goal of natural science." (http-5; 2013-10-16).*

Natural sciences must, by definition be free from all emotional or subjective evaluation and therefore, represent the "**objective truth**". For example, that the sun provides us with a constant source of energy and that the earth revolves around the sun are "objective truths".

But, although there is a gigantic amount of accumulated "objective" scientific knowledge at man's disposal, no scientist would dare lay claim to have access to the ultimate "absolute truth". The reason for this is simple. The more man discovers about the natural world, the more he realizes just how much more there is yet to be discovered. Today's sound and solid knowledge will, in all probability, become inadequate or deficient in the light of tomorrow's discoveries. That means that the knowledge we have discovered up to now, is neither perfect nor complete. For example, some time ago, physicists used to believe in definite cause-effect relationships. But, the theories of Einstein turned all the then existing knowledge on its head. The new acclaimed scientific concept was; relativity. But today, even some of Einstein's theories seem to be challenged by a new concept; the laws of quantum mechanics. Instead of definite cause-effect relations, the scientists prefer to emphasize "probability".

Social Sciences and the "Absolute truth"

The social sciences, such as economics, politics, sociology, etc., in many respects display different characteristics to the natural sciences. Firstly, the social sciences do not and cannot have scientific laws like the natural sciences. In the social sciences laws cannot be applied equally to all countries or communities. Nor can they use the same kind of quantitative analyses. The natural sciences and the social sciences are inherently different. In the social sciences there are too many independent variables to control. Conditions are never the same and cannot be replicated. Different individuals or groups are influenced differently even under similar conditions. In addition, human behavior is always influenced by emotional, environmental or prevalent trends in society. No method is available, to the best of our knowledge, that is capable of reliably measuring the magnitude of the "wants", "desires", "expectations" or the "satisfaction level" of individuals or of different societies. Whatever has been observed and "quantified" by one specific study becomes "history" at the very moment data is collected. Therefore, the neoclassical claim that it is as scientific as the natural sciences is both fallacious and risible.

With regard to the knowledge discovered by the natural sciences, the claim is that there is no "absolute truth". Whatever seems correct at a given time may become obsolete later. This assertion is much more valid and logical when applied to the social sciences. The social sciences cannot replicate any previous event, nor can observations be repeated under the same terms and conditions. Only the, so called "blackboard economists", claim they can magically do this.

The Islamic Faith and the "Absolute Truth"

The Islamic religion is founded upon "faith" like other monotheistic religions. Islamic faith requires the complete acceptance of the teachings and guidance of Allah. Because of this, it is required that one adheres to Allah's commands (farz) and avoid those things that are forbidden (haram). As Kahf says:

> *"The Qur'an was revealed in a manner that responds to incidences, events and affairs as they unfolded in the actual life of the Prophet Muhammad, his companions and his society over the twenty-three year period of revelation. During this period of revelation whenever an event or incidence happened, a few verses of the Qur'an were revealed giving the Shari'ah ruling with regard to such events and incidences." (Kahf; 2013-b).*

The Arabic concept "ilm" (علم) literally means "science" in English. However, the concept has a different meaning in Islamic terminology which refers to "knowledge" of the Quran and Sunnah. Whenever a situation arises where a particular piece of "knowledge" is not found or is not encountered in the proscribed words of the Holy Quran and Sunnah, then it is necessary to apply for guidance to the Islamic jurists (Faqih). The core of jurisprudence is the Quran and the Sunnah. For centuries, since the time of Caliphs', almost all economic issues in Islamic economic thought, emerged from the decrees of this jurisprudence which relies firstly on the Koran and secondly on the Sunnah. On the role of jurisprudence Ashker-Wilson states that:

> *"Wherever there are explicit rules in the Qur'an and the Sunnah, there is no room for self-judgment. But when either is void of an explicit rule, the general understanding of the Qur'anic verses and their purposes and the interpretation of the* Hadith *and their intention, the spirit of the law as we may say, should be used to guide the jurists in arriving at the required rule. No violation to the spirit of the Shari'ah should be committed". (Ashker-Wilson; 2006; 35).*

It is important to note that the Islamic religion does not only teach rituals but regulates all aspects of human life, including one's economic life. There are comprehensive guidelines in the Quran in regard to all human actions, the shaping of social, cultural, political and economic principles and basic everyday legal matters. The ultimate goal is a blessing for mankind. In short, Islam is a total way of life, economic or otherwise.

Islamic Economics and the Notion of "Absolute Truth"

Islam is a total way of life, economic or otherwise. But, does it mean that even the recipes and remedies to "earthly" economic problems are written in its Holy Book? In other words, does the Holy Koran contain the "scientific economic theories" which are designed to assist us in comprehending economic relations specific to this mortal realm, both at national and global level?

If it does, then the recipes and remedies are at hand and all we have to do is to obey the teachings and principles of the Holy Quran. If it doesn't then, we have to look at the Sunnahs in the hope of finding our solutions there.

> *"The Sunnah represents what the Prophet is reported to have said, done and agreed to be undertaken during his lifetime." (Ashker-Wilson; 2006; 33).*

If we find there what we are looking for, then all we have to do is to follow the Sunnah. But, to repeat the question: Can we actually find what we are looking for in the Sunnah?

There is no need to be a well-educated Islamic scholar at the "Mujtahid" level (a scholar who is capable of introducing independently 'new rules or principles' when Muslims face new circumstances that cannot be judged or ruled by the known standards of Shariah), to say that there are no "scientific economic theories" either in the Holy Quran or the Sunnahs. As the matter of fact, nobody expects them to be there. Neither the Quran nor the Sunnah is meant to develop economics as a science. The Holy Quran is a guide book on how to be an obedient servant of Allah, i.e. a faithful Muslim.

So in order to formulate the new rules of jurisprudence leads us inevitably to the third source of Islamic rules and principles: The Islamic jurists (Faqih). In fact this process has occurred for the last 1400 years. As Ashker-Wilson states:

> *"Islamic economic thought has evolved through the development of Islamic law, the Shari'ah. The law incorporates the rules of life for Muslims economically, socially and religiously." (Ashker-Wilson; 2006; 3).*

In the past, economic relationships and their related matters were much easier to handle. Generally whenever there was a dispute, the interested parties sought a remedy according to the Islamic rules and principles determined by the Islamic jurists (Faqih). However, since the Industrial Revolution of the 18th Century, A. Smith founded a new social science called "economics". A. Smith's (et al.) aim was to lay down the foundation stone of economics in order to prove that capitalism is a better economic system than Mercantilism, the dominant economic system at the time.

Since then, economic science has come a long way, so too has its problems. Today's economic problems are highly complex and complicated and require both expert knowledge and experience. Today's economists have to deal with many serious issues ranging from productivity growth under competitive conditions to the actual terms of trade, balance of payments, economic cycles, inflation, unemployment, etc. Kahf points out that:

> *"Driven by a sense of idealism, some of us attribute a special status to the general objectives of the Islamic economic system: Full employment, satisfaction of basic human needs, economic-cum distributive justice, development or improvement in the quality of economic life, economic power, etc. But a closer examination of these objectives indicates us that they are the same for each and all economic systems as usually expressed in their econo-political rhetoric throughout the human history. More specifically, these objectives are also the core objectives of socialism, communism and capitalism even anarchism and all or "isms." The same also arises with regard to the institutions of market, factors of production and the principle of government intervention." (Kahf; 2013-a).*

So both Muslim and non-Muslim economists have to deal, to a large extent, with similar global economic problems. Naturally, the remedies to such economic concerns are of a technical nature rather than an ethical or religious one.

The critical questions are: **Do the Islamic jurists who are trained to be jurists only, have the appropriate knowledge and expertise to deal with today's highly complex problems effectively? Can a Mujtahid come up with more efficient economic solutions than a trained expert economist?**

Chapter-4

An Islamic Value & Price Theory

An alternative approach based on mental labor and technological change

"The Islamic economic paradigm with its new and alternative scientific Islamic economic theories have to be so '**comprehensive**' as well as so perfect in the sense of '**fairness**', '**ethical values**' and '**fruitfulness**', so that when you take out the word 'Islamic', it should appeal to all societies and countries equally, regardless of their religious persuasion."

Hasan Gürak

Introduction

Only lip service was paid to the "growth theory" until the 1950's. Since the 1950s, however, concepts like technological change and mental labor (human capital) have been re-discovered as a vital, essential and indispensable ingredient of the growth theory. Nowadays there is wide a range of endogenous growth theories constructed on the back of these re-discovered concepts. In spite of many shortcomings the trend is promising and may enable modern economists to construct more realistic and reliable growth models capable of accounting for actual global economic facts and developments.

Meanwhile, however, the backbone or the basis of all these theories, i.e., the value and price theory still fails to keep pace with developments in growth theory. It neglects to incorporate key concepts such as technological change and mental labor in its analysis. As a result, the "modern" but sterile price theory is bound to fail to properly account for the price formation in the "real" markets. Nor does it provide any appropriate or sound premises for the construction of any related economic theories that are affected or influenced by the price signals coming from the real markets.

The Hypothesis

The hypothesis of this paper is to show that all value-created or added to the natural resources originates from the labor-power that offers two kinds of services; **mental labor** and **physical labor**. The former, the mental labor, is the original source that constantly introduces "new ideas" that is "new technologies" to transform natural products. Meanwhile the latter, physical labor plays a complementary role in accordance with instructions delivered from the brain. As the paper aims to analyze values and/or prices, all concepts and definitions refer to an exchange-economy in which, the natural resources are accepted as a given and **mental labor is acceded as the genesis and incessant source of all the value created**.

The approach is basically a labor embodied approach, but somewhat distinct from the Classical approaches, including those of Smith, Ricardo and Marx. Though it acknowledges the labor-power as the genesis and a constant source of added value, it makes no claim to be an "invariable" measure nor does it claim that the profit (surplus value) is an "unpaid" or a "surplus" part of labor. In addition, it does not make any claim that proper exchange relations should be based on "equal quantities" of the labor-time employed.

Given demand, new exchange relations are determined by the new conditions created by "new technologies", which are a result of the **productive process of the human mind**, i.e., creative mental labor, cet. par. In other words, the productive faculty of the human mind is assigned a key role in all the exchange relations of relative values and price formation. As Marshall pointed out:

> *Man cannot create material things. ... indeed he may produce new ideas ... his efforts and sacrifices result in changing the form or arrangement of matter to adapt it better for the satisfaction of wants. All that he can do in the physical world is either to readjust matter so to make it more useful, ... or to put it in the way of being made more useful by nature... (Marshall; 1990; 53)*

The emphasis of this analysis is on the "relative" values and prices followed by a brief analysis of the actual market values and prices. The reason for that is not because relative exchange relations provide a better premise for analysis of "actual" price formation but because it has been customary to start with relative values since the time of the Classical economists.

The analysis is "Islamic" because

As far as we know, there has been no "Islamic" "value-price" theory outlined in any economic literature to date. Therefore, western economists are unable to compare this aspect of Islamic economics with their own criteria. There is no evidence that there exists, in any verse of the Koran, pertaining to how prices are to be determined in the marketplace.

> *"Generally, pricing dependent on rules of supply and demand and within the principles of open competition is taken as a criterion. The following answer of the Messenger of Allah to people who resorted to him for controlling current prices and determining the limits of profit is meaningful:* "**Doubtlessly, It is Allah who determines prices, gives abundance and poverty and endows livelihood. I would not like to return to my Lord while one**

of you wants his rights from me because of an injustice in property and life matters." *(Abu Dawud, Buyu 49; Tirmidhi, Buyu 73; Ibn Majah, Tijarat 27)." (http-9).*

Ghazali confirms that incident and says:

> *"Prices rose in Al Madinah during the time of the Messenger of Allah, peace be upon him. People said, '0, Messenger of Allah, prices have gone up. Fix prices for us.' The Messenger of Allah, peace be upon him, said, '**Allah is the Fixer of Prices and the Provider**. I hope to face Allah and no one of you calls me to account for an injustice - for blood or money." (Sahih Al-Bukhari) Monopoly is unheard of in the Islamic market. "No one monopolizes but the blameworthy." (Sahih Muslim) "The one who begets is given, the one who monopolizes is cursed." (Sahih Al- Bukhari)." (Ghazali, 1994; 53).*

However, this does not mean that:

> *"... one can sell things at any price he likes. "Prohibitive price becomes in question when something is sold above the current prices by influencing customers with false swearing, hiding the good's defect, praising the good by attributing to it facilities which it does not really have, showing cost of the production higher than it is and taking advantage of scarcity of the goods. In this sense, the extra profit which is not rightful to the seller is not lawful for him." (http-9).*

Since "value-price" theory is the backbone or the corner stone of all other economic theories, it would naturally be sensible to start by constructing an "Islamic" value-price theory, before attempting to construct other elements of, or an "alternative" to, non-Islamic economic theories. The analysis introduced here i.e., where prices are determined by the competitive market is an attempt to make some contribution to remedy this deficiency.

What makes this particular contribution more Islamic than the other ones? In order to clarify this point, we will first attempt to explain two fundamental Islamic concepts which we hope will provide a bridge between the scientific analysis of price-value and Islamic principles. The first point that should be of note; is that the efforts of the laborer or the "labor-time" spent in order to earn an honest wage are considered as a "sacred" principle in Islamic thought. There is no verse in the Koran or in any Hadith as far as anyone knows which describes or indicates an Islamic wage level. However, as we well know, Islam always praises the "Halal" (permissible) income of the worker.

According to the Turkish Islamic economist Tabakoğlu, labor is the; "... **basic fundamental source of value**" (2008; 68). According to him, because humans are duty bound to oversee and conserve the universe, Islam places a great emphasis on the notion of 'human labor'. (2008; 258). In fact, he claims that:

“**Working is considered equal to Jihad**[11].” (2008; 259) which means, in this context, any kind of activity and behavior used in the service of Allah. In regard to this issue, according to a saying (Hadith) of the Prophet Mohammed: “**Nobody has eaten a more pious morsel than the one earned by human labor**.” (Armağan; 1996; 57). It would not be difficult to establish a close relationship between the “human labor” mentioned in the Hadith and the “human labor” analyzed in this section.

Another important aspect of human labor is its variable quality. As we will see in the analysis below, one of the two fictitious producers, Mustafa, is mentally more creative, and thus more productive than Sasha. This difference, as we know exists in “real life”. Some individuals are simply more productive, more industrious or cleverer than others. This is not contrary to Islamic principles or the Holy Koran, which clearly states that:

> *“It is We Who portion out between them their livelihood in the life of this world: and We raise some of them above others in ranks, so that some may command work from others.” (http-8; 43-32)*

Although the analysis below is not conducted using the standard terminology of Islamic economics, its content is compatible with Islamic principles. One point we should clarify is; the word “creative” when applied to humans, refers to their God- (Allah) -given mental abilities and should in no way be confused with the “creativity of Allah”, as “**the Creator**”. “Human creativity” refers to a human’s (Allah-given) “**ability**” to transform the Allah-created natural resources into useful products. In other words, the creation of the universe by the Creator (Allah) and the invention or “creation” of new man-made products is entirely two completely separate things.

Why Price Theory?

The value or price theory holds a very crucial and central position in economics and has long been considered as the basic tool and as the “essence” of all economic analysis including economic predictions. As is well known, producers as well as consumers, adjust their market behavior according to the price signals, which determine the allocation of their resources. Price signals are capable of influencing

---

11 “Within the context of the classical Islam, particularly the Shiahs beliefs, it refers to struggle against those who do not believe in the Abrahamic God (Allah). However, the word has even wider implications.” http://en.wikipedia.org/wiki/Jihad, 2014-01-16.

crucial variables like the growth rate, inflation, employment, etc. Therefore, it is imperative to have access to a competent price theory, which forms a logical, consistent as well as a reliable basis for all actual transactions. As the "modern" theory fails to satisfy the last condition, a need for an alternative theory arises.

A realistic price theory should not only be capable of explaining exchange ratios, e.g., the relative prices, between two commodities, but also the market prices of all the commodities (tangibles) produced. In addition, this price theory should also be able to explain the pricing system in the intangible service sector, which appears as the neglected "stepchild" of present price theories. Nowadays, the service sector in terms of output and employment accounts for the greater part of the GDP in modern economies, and displays features distinct from the manufacturing sector producing tangible goods.

And, perhaps most important of all, this price theory must be able to account for the past, present and future source of all value generation, the transformation of these values into prices and the distribution of functional income between wages, profits and interest. Only then could one have a more realistic insight into, and a clear interpretation of actual economic relations. Such a theory should also pave the way for the further development of both sound and realistic theories in the related fields like growth, trade, employment, etc.

Towards a New Mindset

As Schumpeter quite rightly pointed out:

> *"....... in practice we mostly do not start from a vision of our own but from the work of our predecessors or from ideas that float in the public mind." (Schumpeter, 1954; 562)*

Throughout this study, the purpose is to escape from the old habituated mindset (thoughts and expressions), which naturally shapes or heavily influences the mindset of any student of economics. This is not an easy task after years or decades of indoctrination. As Keynes, put it:

> *"The difficulty lies, not in the new ideas, but in escaping from the old ones, which ramify, for those brought up as most of us have been, into every corner of our minds." (Keynes; 1973; xxiii).*

In the following sections we will first analyze exchange relations where only physical labor-power is employed in a simple economy. Then, the analysis will concentrate on exchange relations where "creative mental labor" is incorporated into the model of a simple economy, followed by an attempt to convert values into prices.

A Brief Historical Review

In contrast to the "modern" approach, economic science before 1870s was treated more like an interrelated social science. Inexact but actual, rather than exact and fictitious economic relationships were the point of departure. The theory of value was considered to be the backbone of political economy and concepts like "justice" and "equality" which had no place at all in the so called "pure sciences" were not regarded as relevant by a theory claiming to be a "pure science". Extremely abstract mathematical reasoning applied to economic relations, free of any kind of "human weakness" is the result of more than a century of attempts to make economic science an "exact" science like astronomy and physics and economic scholars have come a long way in this respect. British economist Jevons once proudly claimed that his model of exchange relations did;

> *"... not differ in general character from those which are really treated in many branches of physical science". (Blaug; 1990; 147).*

But the models created were nothing but oversimplified idealizations, a hypothetical version of reality, a "fictitious economy". Marshall had foreseen this pathetic trend and warned economists to be cautious in their application of mathematical models and not to transform economic science into a branch of mathematics, but he did not succeed. In time, physical sciences bowed to the developments in science and underwent drastic changes upgrading itself in accordance with the new discoveries arising from Newtonian mechanics and most recently from "quantum" physics, while economics, as a "downgraded" natural science", has remained faithful to its obsolete a priori philosophical criteria.

For many prominent economists, the neoclassical heritage still represents the "**holy grail**" of any analysis capable of revealing the true nature of economic man and his actions. Any dissent from this holy fount of eternal truth is regarded as a grievous error, if not a "mortal" sin. An outside observer can easily get the impression that the neoclassical teaching is the **final frontier** and the **highest stage** of economic thought. Naturally, all scholars do not agree. As Hicks put it:

> *"Pure economics has a remarkable way of producing beavers out of hats -apparently a priori propositions which apparently refer to reality. It is fascinating to try to discover how they got in; for those of us who do not believe in magic must be convinced that they got in somehow." (Hicks; 1983; 367).*

Hicks continues:

> *"Economics is a social study. It is concerned with the operations of human beings, who are not omniscient, and not wholly rational; who (perhaps because they are not wholly rational) have diverse, and not wholly consistent, ends. As such, it cannot be reduced to a pure technics." (Hicks; 1983; 289).*

The critical question is; do we have a logical and consistent alternative theory?

Unfortunately, there seems to be no positive reply to this question, yet. The number of academic units and academicians with "heterodox" orientation has been growing in numbers recently but, there seems to be no widely acknowledged consistent and logical alternative theory, so far. In this section, an attempt will be made to fill this gap based on a different approach based on a distinctive "labor-value" theory which is the basis of all economic theories. Let us begin with the "original" sources of value.

The Original Sources of Value: Nature and Laborer

Let us begin with a definition of "value". In economic terminology, the "value" of a product whether it is a commodity or a service, is the "relative worth" that can either be exchanged for other product(s) (exchange-value) or be used for personal consumption (use-value). The latter is a subjective concept and its magnitude depends, given income, on the ranking of products in accordance with subjective needs and preferences. The former, "exchange-value", expressed in terms of market prices, depends partly on the costs of production and partly on the demand for the specific product, given the competitive environment.

There are only two initial sources of value-generation, the labor-power and nature. Nature provides a wide range of exogenously given and unlabored (unprocessed) objects with use-values. The labor-power adds value to the nature's objects by transforming (reshaping) them, into commercial products containing exchange-values, by utilizing human mental and physical capabilities. In other words, the past and present services of labor-power transform natural products into useful products either for immediate consumption or into inputs of production or into capital goods which in turn are used to increase the productivity of the labor-power.

In a modern society, to initiate a value creation process, the capital owner, e.g., the entrepreneur has to have access to money or capital (savings) to combine (purchase or hire) the material inputs of production such as raw materials, machinery, tools, energy, etc., using the services of labor-power, e.g., mental and physical labor. This feature of savings might give the impression that "capital" is one of the "productive" factors of production; although there is in fact no universally acknowledged definition of "capital" (see Hausman, 1981). In some analyses it appears in monetary form and in others as physical inputs like tools, machinery and sometimes it even refers to both. Both, money-capital and capital goods are the necessary ingredients of production but are certainly not productive ones in the sense that the value adding labor-power or the initial supplier of objects, i.e., nature, are. At first glance, savings seem like a "productive" factor of production as it gives rise to the employment of productive labor-power along with the implements of production. But, money as such, e.g., savings, cannot be productive, as it is not capable of producing any value. Therefore, money is definitely not one of the "productive" factors.

Capital goods are just as productive as savings. Capital goods being the man-made inputs of production help to increase the productivity of the laborer. However, there would be no capital goods unless natural objects were transformed by the laborers. Capital goods can only transfer value to the product at the rate of its depreciation; nothing more, nothing less.

The Labor-power

The labor-power is embodied in products in the form of mental and physical labor, e.g., skilled and unskilled labor. Thus, the labor-power can be defined as;

> *"... the aggregate of those mental and physical capabilities existing in the physical form, the living personality, of a human being, capabilities which he sets in motion whenever he produces a use-value of any kind". (Marx; Vol.I: 270).*

It is the mental component of labor that generates the productive knowledge that accounts for both the quantitative growth and qualitative improvement of physical objects as well as of the services supplied. Physical labor is a necessary ingredient of production but not a sufficient one to increase the added value of nature's produce on its own. Without the contribution of mental labor, it would not be possible to produce the sophisticated goods and services and reach the contemporary standards of living that, some of us all around the globe, so lavishly enjoy. In other words, to possess an exchange value, the contribution of both mental and physical labor, to a more or lesser degree, is imperative at every stage of production. But, while physical labor's contribution is rather limited, the mental labor is capable of continually creating new "added values".

The contributions of mental labor-power (new technologies) can be divided into two groups:

1. **New goods or services** (entirely new ones or old ones in a new form which are usually accompanied by "new" methods of production);
2. **Existing goods and/or services** but employing "new" production processes which reduces the cost per unit output.

Value creation due to new technologies, as indicated above, can also be referred to as **macro-productivity** growth. But, there are, certainly, other methods of increasing the productivity with a "given" technology, which may be referred to as **micro-productivity** growth (see Gürak, 2012 and 2013) which has limited impact in the short term until it reaches optimum levels.

To sum up; it is the mental ability of the labor-power that accounts for ever increasing value creation and sophisticated living standards. But it would have no significance if there were no gifts of nature to be transformed into useful things. Men and nature are, therefore, the two indispensable and inseparable sources, or "**complementary productive factors**", of wealth. And all physical products, no matter how complex and sophisticated, can be considered as arising from to nature's gifts i.e., raw materials, if the input of past and present mental and physical labor content is discounted. Thus, every product may be reduced, in the final analysis, to nature and labor-power.

"Creative" Mental Labor and Value Generation

The crucial and central question in relation to value or price formation is: What are the conditions determining the relative exchange-value of a product? Is it the supply-demand conditions? Is it the labor "embodied" in, or "commanded" by the final products? Or both?

Value Generation - A Simple Model

Below, a simple alternative labor embodied model of value-generation will be presented to see how the "productive knowledge" of the mind (mental labor) enters into the production process and how it effects the exchange relations in terms of relative values.

Let us begin, like Adam Smith did, with the well-known "**hunter model**" and assume two hunters and no tools of production at all, except for the services of labor-power with its two basic faculties, physical and mental labor. Being a quantitative concept, the "physical labor" is easily measurable by terms such as the hours worked, the days needed to complete a task or some other measurable unit while the latter term, the "mental labor", the source of the productive knowledge (new technologies), refers to a subjective concept and is unlikely to be estimated accurately.

Leaving aside, for the time being, this fundamental contribution of mental labor and let us assume that the two hunters in our model work 10 hours a day and the first one, Sasha the deer hunter, acquires 2 deer a day while the second, Mustafa a beaver hunter, acquires 4 beavers a day. If they had lived in a self-sufficient society meaning that all the catch is consumed within the family of each of the hunters respectively, there would be no need to engage in exchange relations. In the absence of exchange relations, there would be no exchange-values, either. But, our hunters do exchange.

Initial Exchange Conditions

Given tastes and preferences, assume that at the end of the day, the two hunters exchange one deer for two beavers, half a day's physical work, which is a fair exchange with respect to the physical labor expended, e.g., 10 hours' work, in each case. Mustafa consumes one deer and two beavers; as does Sasha. Nobody is better or worse off after the exchange, and the supply-demand is in balance after the egalitarian exchange.

Mustafa's supply = 4 beavers = 10 hours' physical labor (1)
Sasha's supply = 2 deer = 10 hours' physical labor (2)
Total supply /per day = 2 deer + 4 beavers = 20 hours' physical labor. (3)
Mustafa's consumption= 1 deer+2 beavers= 10 hours' physical labor (4)
Sasha's consumption= 1 deer+2 beavers=10 hours' physical labor (5)

So far, our two hunters did not make any use of their mental faculties, e.g., mental labor (ML), in their daily work meaning there is no value-added except for the services of the physical labor (PL). Mustafa's ten hours is exchanged for ten hours of Sasha's physical labor. Under the circumstances, the only way to increase the total added value is to extend the hunting time of the physical labor. But by assumption, 10 hours' a day is the limit that can be employed and thus, the total output cannot be increased beyond its present level. The best the community can do is to re-produce the given value the following day. Their prosperity would never improve.

Assume that one day, one of the hunters; say Mustafa, utilizing his mental faculties develops an "idea", a new hunting method (a new technology) which enables him to double the daily catch from 4 beavers to 8 beavers within the same 10 hour time-span. To be more specific, let us assume that he makes some simple tools to assist him in hunting the beavers. Due to the "idea", considered solely in terms of the physical labor time previously needed in trapping 4 beavers, the value of Mustafa's new daily production of 8 beavers would increase from 10 to 20 hours of physical labor, although because of the new "production method" the hours actually employed are still 10.

New total supply/per day = 2 deer+8 beavers = 20 hours PL (6)

But the total value generated is worth 30 hours PL

Or, alternatively

New total supply/day = 20 hours PL+ Mustafa's ML (7)

Mustafa's ML has a daily of worth 10 hours of PL because his catch has doubled. ML denotes "mental labor" or alternatively "productive knowledge", e.g., the new technology, while PL denotes physical labor. Mustafa's mental contribution (new technology) is worth 10 hours of physical labor. In other words, additional-value is worth 10 hours of physical labor and in actual terms it means that Mustafa's productivity has increased by 100 percent a day, in terms of PL. The community has become richer.

What would happen to the exchange relationship with the other hunter Sasha now? Previously, there were 2 deer and 4 beavers in the market. Now, there are 2 deer and 8 beavers. With regard to the new situation, the exchange relations will have to change. What would the new exchange ratios look like?

"Unfair" Equilibrium

<u>Case: 1-A</u>: Following in the footsteps of the Classical economists, one can argue that after Mustafa's mental contribution, it still requires 10 hours' **PL** to catch 2 deer or, alternatively 8 beavers. Equal quantities of labor time are valid for both hunters, and therefore, 1 deer should exchange for 4 beavers instead of 2, in order to maintain the equality of the exchange when considering the labor-time employed. As a result, at the end of the day, Mustafa would be expected to give up 4 beavers which are equal to 5 hours' physical labor in return for 1 deer, which equals Sasha's 5 hours of physical labor a day.

This means that:

Mustafa's consumption should be 1 deer + 4 beavers = 10 hours' PL (8)
Sasha's consumption should be 1 deer + 4 beavers = 10 hours' PL (9)

But in terms of "initial values", each consumes products now worth 15 hours' PL instead of 10. Sasha's 5 hours' physical labor a day could purchase 2 beavers, initially. Now, he can get 4 beavers; double the amount without any contribution on his part to the total wealth of the community.

Is this a "fair" and/or "rational" exchange?

If one ignores the "productivity increasing" contribution of Mustafa's mental labor, exchanging 1 deer for 4 beavers would at first seem like an egalitarian exchange. But as yet Mustafa has not been rewarded for his mental contribution which doubled his productivity and contribution to the common wealth. Instead of a combined value worth 20 hours' PL, there is now a total value which is worth 30 hours PL. Sasha, the other hunter, who made no mental contribution to the common wealth would be the beneficiary of the new exchange relations based on the "physical labor-time consumed" approach. He works only 10 hours but consumes an output value worth 15 hours in terms of the physical labor-time employed. Meanwhile, Mustafa who produces 20 hours value in terms physical labor-time only enjoys 15 hours' output. Such an exchange relationship would not encourage the further development of a new method of productivity, e.g., new technologies, since the system rewards the unproductive person, not the one who enhances the common wealth. In other words, the system is unable to provide any incentives for further value-generation and therefore the new exchange relationships are neither logical nor are they economically rational.

Unequal Exchange

<u>Case: 1-B</u>: Initially, Sasha and Mustafa were exchanging 1 deer for 2 beavers. Assume that after the introduction of the new technology developed by Mustafa, the initial exchange relationships are maintained. Sasha and Mustafa still exchange and consume 1 deer and 2 beavers each. But now, Mustafa has access to an additional 4 beavers which are worth 10 hours' PL, which he can exchange for another product he wants, say for 2 sheep worth 10 hours' PL in another community. Sasha still consumes 1 deer and 2 beavers (equivalent to 10 hours' PL) while Mustafa now has 1 deer, 2 beavers and additional 2 sheep at his disposal for daily consumption. Mustafa's mental contribution entitles him, given the demand, to a higher consumption level. Sasha's standard is unchanged, but the community as a whole is more prosperous.

Mustafa's consumption=1deer+2beavers+2sheep=worth 20 hours' PL (10)

Sasha's consumption =1 deer+2 beavers = worth 10 hours' PL (11)

In this case, there is no egalitarian exchange in the Classical tradition of equal quantities of labor expressed in terms of the time-unit employed. Nevertheless, neither Mustafa nor Sasha consumes less; in fact, there is an increase in total consumption due to Mustafa's mental contribution. This outcome seems to be both, more logical and economically rational, than the foregoing Case:1-A.

A More Likely Outcome

Case: 1-C: If there is an insufficient demand for Mustafa's additional 4 beavers outside his community, then even Sasha might benefit from the new exchange relations and enjoy more consumption. Assume that the community consists only of Sasha and himself and that Mustafa can exchange only 2 beavers for 1 sheep outside his community. Mustafa would now have 6 beavers at his disposal before entering the exchange relations with Sasha, the other member of his community. If the market is to be cleared, Mustafa will have to accept a new exchange relationship where 1 deer is exchanged for 3 beavers. Now, it is not only Mustafa who is better off but so is Sasha who actually made no mental contribution to the increased total supply.

Mustafa's consumption = 1 deer + 3 beavers +1 sheep (12)
Sasha's consumption = 1 deer + 3 beavers (13)

This outcome appear to be closer to reality than the two prior cases, because it allows even the less productive sectors of the economy to benefit from the overall development originating from other "productive" sectors. In other words, it is not only the inherently more dynamic industrial or manufacturing sector which benefit, the service sector, which is prone to a relatively lower productivity growth, can also benefit from a productivity growth in the other sectors.

Different Qualities of Mental Labor

In the simple model presented above, the increase in total wealth was the result of Mustafa's "creative" contribution in the absence of any formal education or training. This creative feature of human mind helps to change and control our environment by creating "new" technologies. Only the human mind possesses the "creative" mental ability necessary to increase the productivity. Mustafa's case was intended to demonstrate mental labor's contribution within the framework of a simple model. Her contribution and the contribution of countless others have been generated and accumulated for many centuries' even millenniums. This accumulated knowledge constitutes an immense pool presently at the service of mankind.

Nobody, no matter how brilliant his/her mental abilities are, acquires the knowledge in the form of "manna from heaven". In our age, knowledge is normally acquired through long years of formal or informal education/training and is enhanced by talent and experience which includes learning-by-doing. Personal abilities as well as the allocation of appropriate socio-economic conditions and opportunities naturally play a significant, if not a determining, role in the final quality of these abilities. Persons who are more fortunate than others in regard to their natural mental endowments or other man-made opportunities naturally acquire a higher degree of qualification than those less fortunate. The laborers are not a homogeneous entity; on the contrary, they are heterogeneous given the inherited natural abilities, they are also influenced by the socio-economic environment.

A contemporary labor force is expected to be able to make the best use of technologically sophisticated and complex production methods. But there is another and more significant contribution expected from the labor-power; that is the introduction of "new" and more advanced technologies. Therefore, it would be more appropriate to analyze the laborer's contribution under two different headings:

1. To maximize output with "given" technologies and resources (efficiency or micro-productivity analysis); and
2. To produce "new" products and/or production methods (technological productivity or macro-productivity analysis).

The impact of macro-productivity is the ever increasing wealth of nations and individuals, while the former, i.e., making the best use of "given" technology and resources, has only a limited impact.

Consequently, we can conclude that, given the natural endowments, the creative capacity of mental labor assisted by physical labor, is the only source of added value to all of the past and present value that has been generated so far and of any future growth. Or, to put it in William Petty's terms;

> *"... labor is the father of material wealth, the earth is its mother." (in Marx;Vol.I; 133-134)*

Keynes, unlike the "Neoclassical-ists" had no problem with this notion.

> *"I sympathise ... with the pre-classical doctrine that everything is produced by labour..... It is preferable to regard labour ... as the sole factor of production." (Keynes; 1991; 213-214).*

Value-Price Relation

How are these values transformed into prices? That was one the central issues troubling the minds of the Classical economists. Ricardo had searched for an "invariable measure" of value to but could not find one, which satisfied him. He claimed that;

> *"... there is no commodity which is not itself exposed to the same variations as the things, the value of which is to be ascertained; that is, there is none which is not subject to require more or less labor for its production." (Ricardo; 1990; 44-45).*

For Marx, using the same exchange-value relations developed by Ricardo, the answer was obvious but Ricardo was unaware of his own discovery. The invariable measure Ricardo was looking for was the services of labor-power, which Marx defined as;

> *"... the aggregate of those mental and physical capabilities existing in the physical form, the living personality." (Marx; Vol. I; 270).*

Marx had attempted to reduce the labor-power with all its physical and mental abilities into a simple quantitative concept in terms of the "socially necessary labor" measurable by the hours consumed and neglecting or overlooking the contribution of "creative" mental labor, which is a result of the labor power's mental abilities. As a result, the exchange relations as in the Case:1 above, where equal quantities of labor time consumed were exchanged, appears to be an egalitarian exchange relation.

As we have seen in the previous sections, given nature's indispensable role in production, the mental labor with its distinctive creative abilities is the only source of our being able to increase value. Therefore, the exchange relations in a proper "relative" value or price theory have to be based on a labor embodied approach with its dual properties, both the mental and physical aspects. Estimation of the actual amount of physical labor consumed is relatively easy to quantify. But, where to find a proper unit of measurement capable of accounting for the contribution of the mental abilities employed is a much more complicated task. Is it in fact a possible task? If there is no unit which we can use to transform these values into prices in a dynamic economy where the introduction of new technologies is a constant process, would demand schedule provide a resolution?

Relative Prices

Value of a product is the "value transmitted" to the product, given the demand for that product. In our simple model in Case:1-A, the relative values were determined by the physical-labor expended. But external demand as in Case:1-B and the external-internal demand relationships as in Case:1-C, showed that the magnitude of the demand is an important element in the determination of relative values. Bearing in mind that the accurate measurement of the value transmitted by the mental labor is highly unlikely, the relative market prices will be "assumed" to reflect the values transmitted and the magnitude of the demand. It is important to note that relative price ratios do not reflect actual transactions in a monetary economy accurately. But they can be used as a tool to demonstrate the crucial role of the mental contribution, in the form of "new" technology, in the formation of emerging new price levels, given the demand.

Case: 2-A (as presented above)

Let us start by reconsidering our simple economy with two hunters and introduce money as the sole medium of exchange in their transactions. Ignoring aspects like risk and profit for the sake of simplicity, and assume that one deer is worth 30 $ and one beaver 15 $. Initial exchange relations based on 10 hours' physical labor a day can be expressed as follows:

$$2\text{ (deer)} * 30\ \$ = 4\text{ (beavers)} * 15\ \$ \qquad (14)$$

Where;

$$1\text{ deer} = 2\text{ beavers} \qquad (15)$$

Or

$$30\ \$ = 2 * 15\ \$ \qquad (16)$$

Now, let us assume once again that Mustafa, the beaver hunter, utilizing his mental faculties, develops a new hunting method which doubles his productivity from 4 to 8 beavers within the same time-span of 10-hours. Disregarding any reward for Mustafa for his productive contribution, and estimating the value created by labor in terms of the time-units consumed, the new exchange relation between Sasha and Mustafa would be as follows:

$$2\text{ (deer)} * 30\ \$ = 8\text{ (beavers)} * 7.5\ \$ \qquad (17)$$

Where;

$$1\text{ deer} = 4\text{ beavers} \qquad (18)$$

Or;

$$30\ \$ = 4 * 7.5\ \$ \qquad (19)$$

In terms of initial prices, Sasha's total labor valued at 30 $ now commands a 4 beaver value of 60 $. Is this a "fair", "logical" and/or "rational" exchange relation?

The equal labor-time approach to exchange rewards the less productive hunter, Sasha, and penalizes the more productive Mustafa. Under these circumstances, there would be no incentive for Mustafa to make any effort to further improve his productivity. Naturally, a person might also be driven by motives other than financial reward. But for the sake of argument, we shall ignore such cases.

Case: 2-B

Given the initial price and demand where 1 deer is exchanged for 2 beavers, Mustafa, the more productive hunter, could be in a better-off position if he can sell the additional 4 beavers in other markets. Given a demand by a third party consumer at the initial price of the beavers (15 $ each), Mustafa's total income could increase from 60 $ to 120 $ a day, while that of Sasha, the less productive one, remains at 60 $ a day.

Mustafa's income= 1 deer (30 $) + 6 beavers (6 * 15 $)= 120 $ (20)
Sasha's income= 1 deer (30 $) + 2 beavers (2 * 15 $)= 60 $ (21)

Meanwhile, the total income of both, Sasha and Mustafa, would increase from 120 $ to 180 $ thanks to the contribution of Mustafa's productive mental abilities. Mustafa's greater income is the result of and a justified reward for his intellectual contribution, e.g., productivity growth.

New total income/per day= 8 beavers*15$ + 2 deer*30$ = 180 $ (22)

The prices have remained unchanged i.e., at the initial level due to a sustained demand from third party sources outside the original community.

Case: 2-C

Suppose that the external demand is such that it causes the price of one beaver to decline from 15 $ to 10 $. As a result, and in order to clear the markets, one deer will have to be exchanged for 3 beavers in our original community. The new but somewhat deteriorated exchange ratio for Mustafa would be as follows:

1 (deer) * 30 $ = 3 (beavers) * 10 $ (23)

Plus two beavers worth 20 $ sold at external markets.

Mustafa's new income = 6 * 10 $ + 2 * 10$ = 80 $ (24)

Total income =Mustafa's income 80 \$+Sasha's income 60 \$=140 \$ (25)

Sasha now consumes 3 beavers instead of 2, a 50 % improvement in his consumption. Sasha and Mustafa's joint total income is now 140 \$. As a result, the deer hunter benefits from Mustafa's mental contribution but Mustafa end up with deterioration in terms of trade. On the other hand, both Mustafa and Sasha are now better off.

Relative Prices in the Service Sector

In the view of many Classical economists including Marx, the output of the service sector was considered as "unproductive". But, in the modern economies, it is an acknowledged and quantitatively proven fact that the service sector output is not only productive (value-producing) but also constitutes the largest share of GDP or GNP. There is nothing tangible or storable produced by the service sector, as is produced in the industrial sectors. Thus, there are no physical quantities to exchange as in the simple model above. In commodity production, there is a close relationship between the "tangible" input and "tangible" output, which normally move in the same direction. In other words, with given fixed costs, each unit output's cost is closely related to cost of the material inputs. In contrast, the service sector output is characterized by a higher intensity in the labor-power services. Unit costs are closely related to labor-power costs as a function of the time consumed, given the initial fixed cost and capital-goods cost. For instance, a teacher, a hairdresser, a business consultant or a musician can increase the total amount of the service they supply by working longer hours per day or week or month given the initial combination of the physical inputs which they employ.

By reducing the contribution of the labor inputs into a standard measurable unit such as the "labor-time-consumed" might appear to be an appropriate method with which to analyze the relative values or the prices used in the service sector. But, if we take into consideration the different qualities of mental labor required in producing the different kinds of the services that are required, such comparisons lose all their credibility. The value or price of the variable quality of the labor services will of course be different for each type of the service demanded. Thus, the value or price of each specific labor service would be different, even if the "equal labor time-consumed" unit was used in calculating the price or value of the supply for each individual service. Despite its significance for all national economies, a separate value/price analysis in the service sector will not be undertaken in this article, because of the limited scope of this article.

Commodity Sector Price Formation

So far, the analysis was focused on the creation and exchange of **relative-values or prices** in the commodity producing (tangible) sector. But, the analysis fails to reflect the real situation adequately; because the role of profit involved in the production process, in price formation and in exchange relationships have been neglected. In this part, profit will be introduced into the price formation analysis as it would occur in a monetary exchange economy. Introducing profits would inevitably lead to the simultaneous study of functional income distribution, which, however, will not be undertaken at this time due to limited space. The formation of new prices after the introduction of new technologies will be dealt with only briefly, again as a result of limited space.

Transformation of Values into Prices

A Case of "Barter-Exchange"

In barter exchange relations as in the simple model previously presented, the exchange-value of each product was determined by the mental and physical labor embodied in it i.e., (**LE**), the objective value (**OV**), the magnitude of demand for the product (**D**), and the subjective value (**SV**), which was previously assumed to be a "given". The last (**SV**) reflected the value that the end-users are willing to give up in exchange for a desired product, while the objective value, **OV**, reflected the value of the past ($\mathbf{LE}_{t-1}$) and the present ($\mathbf{LE}_t$) mental and physical labor embodied in the product (**LE**), excluding any or all profits.

Initially, one deer was exchanged for two beavers. But after a mental contribution, Mustafa's acquisitions had doubled and in order to clear the market, one deer had to be exchanged for four beavers, as in Case:1-A and Case:2-A.

In Case:1-B and Case:2-B, there was a demand for an additional four beavers which originated outside the community and as a result, Mustafa's income doubled. From a more realistic and rational "exchange relation" perspective, which is found in Case: 1-C and Case: 2-C, both members of the community benefited from Mustafa's mental contribution, but Mustafa's profit was higher than Sasha's. All these factors indicated that the market exchange-value (**MV**) of a product is determined by the **LE** and D. Thus, in the absence of profit, the **MV** equation can be shown as:

$$MV = f\,(OV; SV) \qquad (26)$$

Or, alternatively

$$MV = f(LE; D) \tag{27}$$

implying that **LE** is the sole source of any value generation, while **D** gives the final shape to the exchange relationships by means of "haggling and bargaining". There were no profits involved and exchange was based on equal quantities of **MVs**, as in Case:1-C.

$$\mathbf{1\ MV^{d} = 3\ MV^{b}} \tag{28}$$

Instead of the initial

$$\mathbf{1\ MV^{d} = 2\ MV^{b}} \tag{29}$$

$\mathbf{MV^{d}}$ and $\mathbf{MV^{b}}$ denote the market values of deer and beaver, respectively. The critical question in these relative exchange relationships is: How to transform these values into market prices (MPs) in the "barter" exchange?

To obtain the **MP** we simply have to add any profits ($\boldsymbol{\pi}$) to both sides of the equation used in the exchange relationships. Since profit rates are expected to be equal as a result of competition, new exchange relationships would not affect the essential exchange and be based upon, in a sense, the original **MV**s of deer and beaver respectively.

$$\mathbf{MP^{d} = MV^{d} + \pi^{d}} \qquad \text{one deer's MP} \tag{30}$$

$$\mathbf{MP^{b} = MV^{b} + \pi^{b}} \qquad \text{one beaver's MP} \tag{31}$$

$$\boldsymbol{\pi} = \mathbf{f\,(SV)} \qquad \text{or} \qquad \boldsymbol{\pi} = f\,(D) \tag{32}$$

And, given Case:1-C:

$$1MV^{d} + \boldsymbol{\pi}^{d} = 3\ MV^{b} + \boldsymbol{\pi}^{b} \tag{33}$$

By assumption;

$$\boldsymbol{\pi}^{d} = \boldsymbol{\pi}^{b} \tag{34}$$

Then,

$$1MV^{d} = 3\ MV^{b}$$

As in (Eq.28), or, alternatively

$$\mathbf{1MP^{d} = 3\ MP^{b}} \tag{35}$$

In other words, in a "barter" exchange model **MPs** deviate from **MV**s only to the extent of the size of the profits. Since profit rates are assumed to be uniform, **MPs** would reflect actual **MV**s. But, as we all know, barter exchange is a rare exception in modern economies.

Price Formation in a Monetary Economy

In monetary economies, given a fair competitive environment and an appropriate institutional and cultural setting, prices are determined by each firm in every sector on the initial costs plus a mark-up basis in accordance with long term profit maximization goals, given the level of demand. Costs include the prices of all the inputs of production including any profits along with the present wage level. There are no homogeneous products and thus no uniform price, even within the same sectors or sub-sectors. Accordingly, there are no homogeneous production methods, either. Each product can be produced by a different production method and displays unique product-specific features. In other words, each firm may require labor-power services as well as financial, organizational and technological settings in different qualities and quantities. Given these features, each firm would have different break-even points and different optimum plant capacities. As distinct from the simple model above, we have to bear in mind that there may be at least one additional input of production other than the input of the labor-power services.

Although labor-power is the sole source of all value generation, as before, the **MP** paid by end-users normally exceeds the value transmitted to the product. The reason for the difference is the "**profit**" (**π**) paid to the entrepreneur for the "**risk**" he/she assumed. This is not payment for a value transmitted to the product by capital. In fact, it is a payment "in excess" of the costs. In a sense, it is a "**surplus cost**" but not an "**unpaid surplus value**" to labor-power because the labor-power receives pre-determined wages in return of their services. This additional payment or "**surplus cost**" is a necessary and indispensable ingredient so that the capitalist system can keep functioning. Thus, the **MP** can be defined as "**the monetary expression of a product regulated by CP plus π which is shaped by D**".

Assume an economy where labor-power is the only input of production of a Commodity-X. Given **D**, the cost of production (**CP**) of **X** would be determined by;

$$\mathbf{CP^x = w * L} \tag{36}$$

And;

$$MP^x = CP^x + \pi^x \tag{37}$$

In this initial stage of production with "labor-power input only", the **MV** of a product equals the **CP**, while the MP is greater than the MV (**MP > MV**) by virtue of the size of the "profit". In other words, whenever profits are introduced, neither **CP** nor **MV** would no longer reflect the true **MP** of the product.

Production with Multiple Inputs

Assume that Commodity-**X** produced yesterday is used as an input in the supply of Commodity-**Y** today. The **CP** of **Y** would comprise of past and present **w*L** plus the past $\boldsymbol{\pi}$ acquired;

$$CP^{y} = w^{x} * L^{x} + \boldsymbol{\pi}^{x} + w^{y} * L^{y} \quad (38)$$

But,

$$MV^{y} = w^{x} * L^{x} + w^{y} * L^{y} \quad (39)$$

And, bearing in mind that **D** affects both $\boldsymbol{\pi}$ and the relative exchange ratios as in the simple model;

$$MP^{y} = w^{x} * L^{x} + \boldsymbol{\pi}^{x} + w^{y} * L^{y} + \boldsymbol{\pi}^{y} \quad (40)$$

To put it differently;

$$MP^{y} = CP^{y} + \boldsymbol{\pi}^{y} \quad (41)$$

Where,

$MP^{y} > MV^{y}$ by the amount of $\boldsymbol{\pi}^{x} + \boldsymbol{\pi}^{y}$

Alternatively;

$$MP_{t} = wL_{t-1} + \boldsymbol{\pi}_{t-1} + wL_{t} + \boldsymbol{\pi}_{t} \quad (42)$$

t denotes the time.
In regard to a product with "**n**" inputs, the **MV** and **MP** would be:

$$\mathbf{MV}_{n} = \Sigma\, \mathbf{LE}_{n} \quad (43)$$

$$\mathbf{MP}_{n} = \boldsymbol{\Sigma}\, \mathbf{LE}_{n} + \boldsymbol{\Sigma}\, \boldsymbol{\pi}_{n} \quad (44)$$

There is a break-even price level (**B**) where cost equals income. However, producers guided by long term profit motive would be reluctant to produce at price **B**, at least, not in the long term. Although **MP** always includes payment in excess of the **MV** of a product under normal conditions, the exchange of two producer-consumers, like Mustafa and Sasha, might present a different and interesting result. The producers would be exchanging equal quantities of **MV**s among themselves in a "**barter-like**" manner. In other words, since $\mathbf{p}^{a}=\mathbf{p}^{b}$, then $\mathbf{CP}^{a}=\mathbf{CP}^{b}$ and accordingly, $\mathbf{MP}^{a}=\mathbf{MP}^{b}$. In this sense, they would be paying the break-even price, without making profits.

Meanwhile, however, the rest, or the non-capitalist end-users, have to pay profits in excess of **CP** for the system to function, which leads to different implications with regard to income distribution. It implies that some value above and beyond the production cost is being created by the non-capital-owners for the capital-owners.

Now, in the light of above arguments, the relevant and critical question is; where to set the **MP** in a competitive market for a given product with regard to the mental contribution, e.g., the technological innovations? Below, three different cases of price formation will be studied.

1. **A Given** product and a **given** technology (production method):
2. **A Given** product but a **new** production method introduced by mental labor:
3. **New** products supplied by **new** production methods.

A "Given" Product & a "given Production Method" & Profit

Let us first consider a case with a **given** technology embodied in the capital goods disregarding all non-profit motives. Given optimum plant capacity with a **CP** schedule and assuming optimum micro-productivity, i.e., optimum allocation of the inputs of production, the rate of profit (**r**) would be determined by **MP** set on a (**CP**+π) basis where π would be subject to the magnitude of demand (**D**). Or, to put it differently, the projected size or rate of profit by the firm would determine the **MP** and the quantity demanded or supplied (**q**), given the **PC** and the **CP**-schedule.

Figure-1 shows the relationship between the quantities supplied and profits with a given plant capacity. **B** denotes the break-even point of production where average unit costs equal the average unit returns, resulting in no profits. The size as well as the rate of the profit per unit output would increase as the total quantity supplied moves to the right of **q** towards **q***. Given **D**, at the maximum output level (**q***) determined by the plant capacity, the size and rate of profit would be at the highest possible level.

Assuming a uniform price for a product in a specific sector and "given" but "heterogeneous" production methods, **CP**-schedules and plant capacities. Profit rate for each firm might differ from the average profit rate in the sector as the quantities demanded or supplied vary from firm to firm, cet. par. In other words, similar products produced by different types of technologies would naturally produce different unit production costs, optimum plant sizes, break-even points and size or rate of profits. Differing levels of the quantities produced would also influence the size and rate of profits.

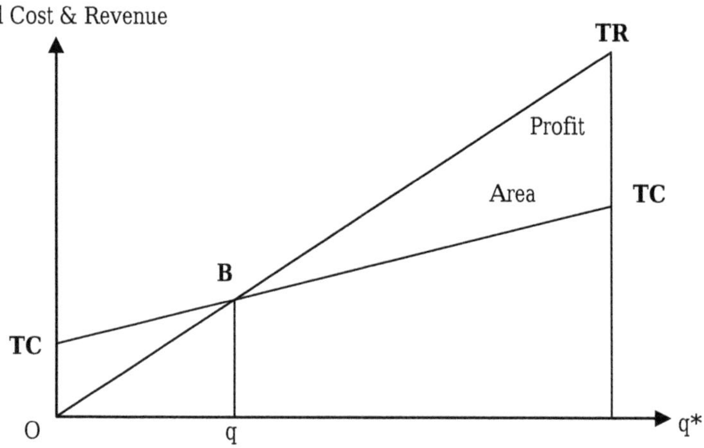

Figure: 1

How Influential is Variations in Demand?

Assume that the **MP** is initially set at a level, which assured a sufficient demand for full plant capacity utilization. But, then, for some reason the demand curve shifts towards the origin, from $\mathbf{D_1D_1}$ to $\mathbf{D_2D_2}$. Given the **MP** and full plant output capacity by **q***, as in Figure-2, the shift in the demand curve would cause alterations not only in the quantities produced but also in the size and rate of the profits. The profit would follow a decline in **D** and drop from the area of the quadrilateral "**abcd**", to the area of "**abB**", also causing a decline in the quantity produced by the gap of $\mathbf{q^1q^x}$, e.g., $\mathbf{Oq^x–Oq^1}$. The new but inefficient capacity utilization level is denoted by the dashed line $\mathbf{aq^1}$. At that level, both the size as well as the rate of profit would be lower.

Following the decline in demand and the ensuing excess plant capacity, the firm may respond by changing its price. If the **MP** is increased, the revenue line **OTR** would become steeper, $\mathbf{OTR^1}$, but it would be unlikely to restore the initial profit size and full plant capacity level (Figure:3). If the **MP** is reduced in response to a fall in the demand curve, the **OTR** revenue line would become flatter; $\mathbf{OTR^2}$, and the plant capacity utilization would increase, if the end-users respond by increasing their demand. But the restoration of the initial profit level would be impossible.

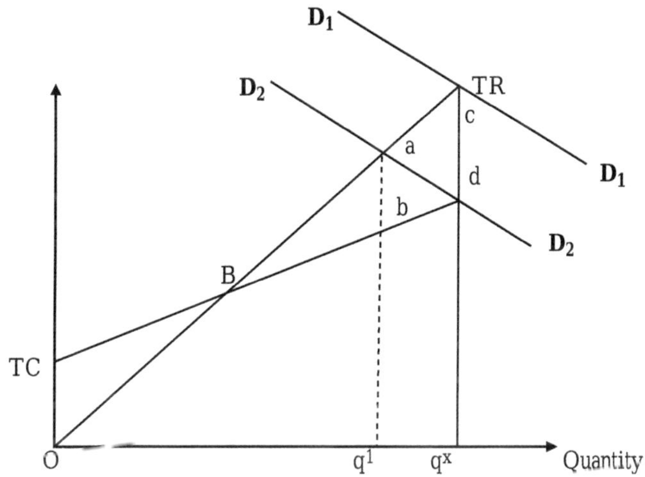

Figure: 2 Total Cost & Revenue

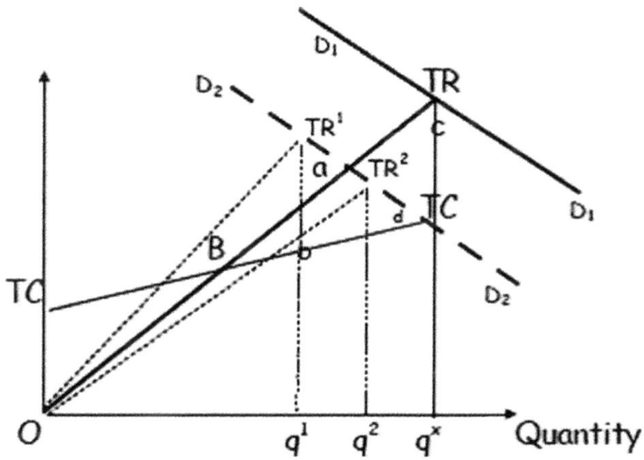

Figure: 3

To conclude; the labor-embodied (**LE**) argument alone falls short of explaining the market prices, especially in the case of a supply-demand imbalance. **CP**, which reflects (past and present) **LE** and past π seems to regulate the minimum **MP**- level, which, in the final stage, is adjusted by the "haggling and bargaining" in the market. Thus, fluctuations in demand causing imbalance in supply-demand conditions have an influential impact on the determination of the short term **MP**. With a "given" technology and a supply-demand balance, the long term **MP** is more likely to reflect the **LE** and past **π**, plus the present **π** shaped by present **D**-schedule. But, there is a crucial reality; technology (mental contribution) is not a static "given", on the contrary, it is continually changing.

Technological- (Macro-) Productivity Growth & Profit

The major distinction of the following analysis is the introduction of "new" technologies, which are the products of the creative mental labor. By assumption, in this analysis the demand is a given" and there is no excess plant capacity.

A "Given" product but "new" production method and price

There are two motives for a profit driven firm to produce a "given" product with a "new" technology; either (a) to make higher profits by reducing unit **CP**, and/or (b) to become more price-competitive. After the introduction of new method; the **expected** and normally **realized** rate of profit should be higher than before, at least until the others catch up. Figure:4 shows a hypothetical case of declining costs and increasing profits in relation to a cost-saving technological change with a given output. **TC**^{x} - **TC**^{x} line indicates the new cost curve, which is now closer to the origin as a result of the new method indicating lower production costs, thus higher profits. The new profit area is **acB**^{x} where **acB**^{x}>**ab**B. The profit area before the introduction of the new technology (productive knowledge) is indicated by the triangle **abB.**

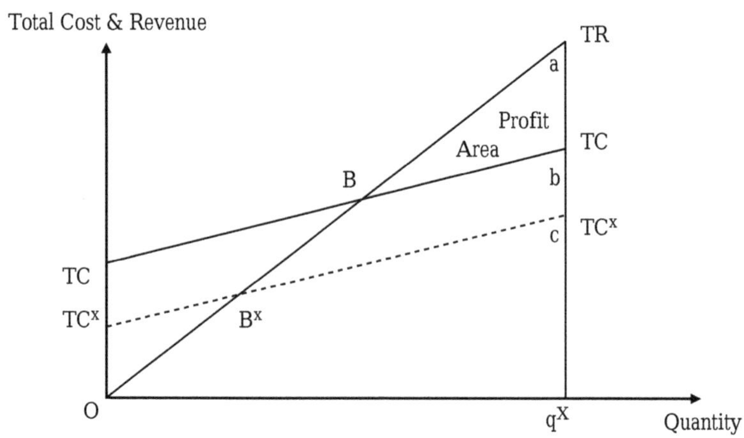

Figure: 4

If the "new" technology facilitates an increased supply with "given" inputs, then, again, the size and the rate of profits would increase, cet. par. (Figure:5). The new plant capacity is denoted by **Oq**^{xx} while **BTR**^{xx} **TC**^{xx} denotes the new profit area, which is larger than **BTRTC**. The new situation also implies a lower **CP** per unit output as the share of fixed costs in the per unit output declines.

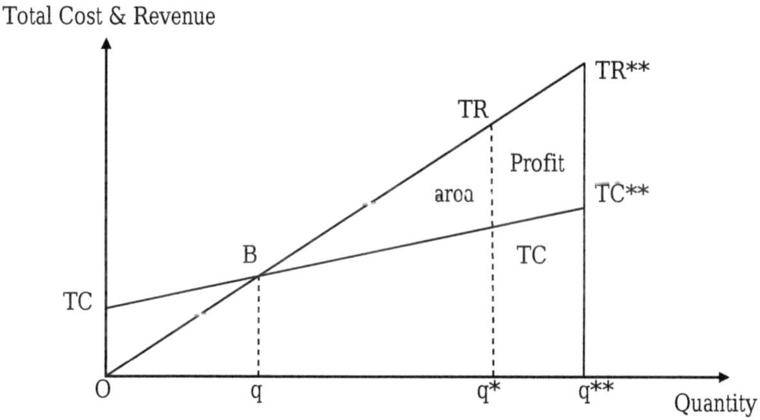

Figure: 5

Now that the unit production costs are lower, will the price remain unchanged?

If there is a sustained demand at the initial price level, there would be no need to change the price, as shown in the Cases 1-B and 2-B in the simple relative exchange model with our two hunters. As a result of new technology, the size and the rate of profits would increase. If the firm wants to improve its competitive position, then it would have to lower the price. The long term targets of firms would determine the limit of price decline. Reducing the price until the previous level of profit rate is restored would not be an irrational behavior, cet. par.

Conclusion; as a result of the creative mental labor's contribution, the new price level will have to be set somewhere between the prevailing **MP** and a lower level above break-even price in accordance with firm's short and long term targets and the magnitude of demand.

"New" products, price & profit

The distinctive feature of economies is the continuous introduction of "new" products as well as new production methods, which appears to have accelerated in the present so called "the age of knowledge". Since both, the products as well as the production methods are **new**; there would be no preceding price level with which to make a comparison. In other words, a study of the effect of the price of a **new technology** on a **new product or production method** would only give us information on the "new" sets of prices. It can be claimed, however, without any hesitation, that the **expected**, and normally the **realized**, profit rate would be higher than the prevailing average market rate, because the owner of the new technology would enjoy a monopolistic power in the market, until the competitors catch up.

Concluding Remarks

The purpose of this paper was to display the genesis of and the ever changing source of "added value". The analysis so far has indicated that, given natural resources and physical labor, **the creative knowledge of labor-power** is **the sole source of all the exchange-values created and all the wealth which is accu**mulated. Price is determined by three factors; cost of production, profit rate and demand.

In a capitalist market economy where money is used as the medium of exchange, the capital-owners obtain a part of the sale-price referred to as "profit". What capital-owners receive as profit is not a part of the income generated by capital-owners. It is a part of the added value paid to capital-owners (investors) as a reward the risks they have assumed in the supply of these goods and services, which is both legitimate and necessary for the smooth functioning of markets to enable them to supply the products which are in demand.

The rate of profit always affects the sale price directly and influences the trend of demand. On the other hand, the degree of demand may in turn influence the sale-price of products as well. To put it another way, the sale-price influences the level of demand while the level of demand may influence the sale-price; there is a reciprocal interaction.

All commodities are originally the product of nature transformed or re-shaped by labor-power. Given the limited impact of the physical labor, the creative mental faculty of labor-power continually introduces new ideas in order to change and control our environment, which in its turn changes our entire way of life. Assuming an optimum resource (micro-economic) efficiency in production, mental labor's "new" contribution that is "new" technology influences the price-level by introducing either;

1. a cost-saving "new" method of production, "given" the product; or
2. "new" products with "new" sets of values and prices.

In the first case, the potential profit rate, and in the second, the expected, and the usually realized, profit rate is higher than the average rate.

Unequal distribution of income has always been a major problem area and an embarrassment for both economic science and economists. The analysis above indicates that this problem can be tackled, at least to some extent, by increasing the number of persons in a "barter-like" exchange, that is by making people "profit receivers" who exchange products with profits instead of being just wage-earners who have to pay in excess of the value transmitted to products. In a society where everybody receives an "equal" share of profits, income distribution would be much fairer, though not at an optimum level.

Chapter-5

On the Islamic Theory of Trade

Introduction

According to Islam, "honest" tradesmen are, in a way, a blessed group of businessmen. The Prophet Muhammad was a successful tradesman until the age of about forty. The Caliphs Abu Bakr, Omar and Utman were also tradesmen and belonged to the distinguished families of Mecca. Thus, trading and trade related economic activities dominated the economic life of Mecca, the city of pilgrimage placed at the crossroads of the trade routes. Other types of economic activities such as craftsmanship and farming were practiced but did not have much chance to progress in the desert.

> *"The essence of commerce is sincerity, safety, well comprehension of the age and utmost kindness and utmost decency shown towards customers. One who lacks one of them actually causes damage to the essence of commerce and thus blocks his own livelihood." (http-9).*

All parties involved in an exchange transaction have to agree on the exchange terms and nobody should be left discontented. The Koranic verse entitled "Nisa", says:

> *"O ye who believe! Eat not up your property among yourselves in vanities: But let there be amongst you traffic and trade by mutual good-will" (Women 4/29).*

It clearly states that, there must be some form of mutual good-will among the parties involved in the exchange relationship. However, it is important to note that the "mutual good-will" does not make an "unfair" exchange permissible. Cheating or earning impermissible income is forbidden (Haram) and considered an atrocity.

> *"God hath permitted trade and forbidden usury." (The Cow; al-Baqarah, 2:275).*

There is no limit set for the profit rate but it does not mean that the tradesman can sell his product at any price he wants. Restrictive practices may have to be put in place in order to protect the buyer. Therefore, tradesmen should not be too greedy in their transactions. The Prophet warned the tradesmen who remonstrated with him regarding the controlling of current prices:

> *"Doubtlessly, It is Allah who determines prices, gives abundance and poverty and endows livelihood. I would not like to return to my Lord while one of you wants his rights from me because of an injustice in property and life matters." (Abu Dawud, Buyu 49; Tirmidhi, Buyu 73; Ibn Majah, Tijarat 27) (http-9).*

The Muslim tradesmen are encouraged to enter into commerce at any time, even on the Day of Prayer, Friday. The Koranic verse "Friday" says:

"O ye who believe! When the call is proclaimed to prayer on Friday (the Day of Assembly), hasten earnestly to the Remembrance of Allah, and leave off business (and traffic): That is best for you if ye but knew!

And when the Prayer is finished, then may ye disperse through the land, and seek of the Bounty of Allah. and celebrate the Praises of Allah often (and without stint): that ye may prosper." (Friday; 62; 9-10) (http-10).

When asked about the best way to make a living, the Prophet answered:

"**It is one's elbow grease and acceptable trade.**" *(Ahmad bin Hanbal, Musnad, 3/466). And this refers to trade in which there are no betrayal and lying. (http-9).*

In another occasion, the Prophet is believed to have said that; "**nine tenths of livelihood comes from trade**." (http-9).

The Prophet also had some advice for the tradesman and good news for the honest tradesmen:

"A tradesman who is straight (honest) both in his words and actions is in the shadow of the sky on the Day of Judgment." (Ibn Majah, Commerce 1) […] "A tradesman who is reliable in his words and actions is with prophets, the siddiq and martyrs." (Tirmidhi, Buyu 4; Ibn Majah, Tijarat 1). (http-9).

There are some essential modes of behavior expected from Muslim tradesmen and are prescribed in the Koranic verses or the Sunnah. These can be stated briefly as;

- Starting the business transaction by invoking the name of Allah.
- Aiming to earn a permissible (Halal) income.
- Not hiding any defect of the product.
- Avoiding any interest (riba).
- Avoiding any attempt which would influence the market price.
- Avoiding black-market transactions.

If summarized in one single sentence; the Muslim tradesman must avoid Haram and only strive after permissible income.

For hundreds of years, Islamic scholars have been referring, in their "fatwas", to the ethical issues related to trading activities and the expected behavior of Muslim tradesmen, based on the Koranic verses and the Sunnah. Despite the fact that the Prophet himself and the successive three Caliphs had been practicing traders in their time and that tradesmen in general have never been sidelined in economic activities in countries under Islamic rule, Islamic scholars and economists have not introduced a 'universal' or 'global' trade theory which is able to outline the pros and cons of Islamic trade principles that could be applied either to individual enterprises or national economies even in non-Muslim countries.

There is no Islamic economic theory of trade in the Holy Book or the Hadith. This comes as no surprise; after all, neither the Koranic verses nor the Hadiths are meant to be scientific economic textbooks.

What could be the underlying reasons behind this ignorance or neglect by Islamic scholars and economists in their failure to develop a viable trade theory?

If they assumed that someday all individuals and nations will convert to Islam and there will be no need for a universal or global theory of trade, their assumptions was wrong. As the majority of world population is non-Muslim, surely Islamic economists should have a rational message to the non-Muslim world about how one should conduct one's trading relationships.

Developing a New Theory of Trade

It is difficult to understand why the Islamic economists have never attempted to develop an essentially Islamic theory of trade. It seems like a void in Islamic economic thinking, not to have access to a universally or globally applicable Islamic trade theory. If there were such a theory would it not be useful in demonstrating to the non-Muslim world the benefits of Islamic trade relationships? Moreover, the non-Muslim world would be able to get a better insight into the ethical codes determining the behavior of Muslim tradesmen that are so highly praised and encouraged by their fellow Muslims.

Unfortunately, no alternative trade theory that is in harmony with Islamic teachings has been developed so far. But it does not mean that it is too late to develop one. Hopefully the Islamic economists will increase their scientific efforts in order to fill in this void. In order to achieve this goal, they appear to have three options:

1. Adopt, adjust and further develop existing Western trade theories to conform to Islamic values.
2. To accept one or more of the existing theories developed by the Western secular economists.
3. To develop an entirely "new" valid and universally applicable Islamic theory of trade.

On Western Trade Theories

Let us consider first the likelihood of a successful adoption of an existing theory of trade introduced and developed by Western secular economists.

Economic theories about global trade, (international trade, world trade, and foreign trade, what you will) are believed to have started with A. Smith's view of an "**absolute advantage**" principle. However, it was soon realized that the products of the relatively more advanced industrial countries had an "absolute advantage" in all areas, over those products produced by enterprises in the less developed countries. Based on the "absolute advantage" principle, the products of less developed countries had no chance to compete. The "absolute advantage" principle of A. Smith was correct but it did not serve the interests of the Western producers to promote global "free trade".

However, D. Ricardo's "**comparative advantage**" concept came to the rescue. According to this new "ideology", all countries could enter into a global free trade relationship and benefit. As time passed, many other contributions followed to promote this global "free trade". The good news was; regardless of the development level, all countries would benefit from this free trade. Some of the new concepts introduced to promote global free trade can be summarized thus; "offer curves", "opportunity cost" and "factor endowments". Later we observe some new attempts based on concepts like "technological difference", "human-capital", "product cycle" and "revealed comparative advantages".

However, none of the preceding international trade theories appeared successful in presenting a comprehensive theory that was capable of reflecting actual economic relations and transactions. The reason for this was that their initial starting point was based on unrealistic assumptions and fictitious relationships. These economic models could not go beyond the point of being a study in the realm of "blackboard economics". These economists referred to trade between different "countries" in their economic models. In doing this, they also made a big mistake; in reality, it is not "**countries" that engage in trade"; it is the "enterprises" within the different countries which engage in trade**. Trade between countries is in fact trade between the enterprises of the different countries.

Another problem with the Western trade theories is Ricardo's principle of "**comparative advantage**", i.e., the comparative abilities of nations according to "**opportunity costs**". Being a purely "ideological" principle, it is merely a face-saving ploy used by economists defending global free trade. Since, in reality, it is the enterprises not the countries that trade, no rational, profit-motive driven enterprise would pursue economic relations with other enterprises based on the principle of comparative advantage, except, possibly, for those in a trading relationship with Soviet type economies. An "ideology-free" rationale clearly demonstrates that global exchange relationships are governed by the principle of "**absolute advantage**", i.e., the comparative abilities of enterprises in accordance with the principles of "**absolute costs and competitive market prices**". There is no need for a comprehensive and in depth trade analysis in order to discover this fact; simply go and ask any enterprise manager engaged in international trade and he/she will tell you what the reality actually is.

The following pertinent questions might pop up:

1. Assuming that the inadequacy of foreign trade theories based on "comparative advantage" is so obvious, how come nobody has discovered it before?
2. Why should the use of the term "foreign trade" be considered a mistake, since the export earnings are registered in a country's trade balance sheets?

The answer to the first question is simple; in most of the economics departments of universities around the world, the Anglo-Saxon ideology is the dominant one. Let us recall: A. Smith had formulated his trade model with two countries and two products using the "absolute advantage" principle. But in the case that one of the two trading countries had an absolute advantage in both sectors, as occurs in reality, there would be no motive for the disadvantaged country to enter into a free trade relationship with it. Ricardo's law of "comparative advantage" arrived just in time to rescue this Anglo-Saxon foreign trade theory. In the case that one country has absolute advantage in both sectors, in a two-country, two goods model, the comparative advantage principle would make foreign trade, at least in theory, look like a rational and mutually beneficial process. The economists promoting global free trade highly admired this approach and dedicated themselves to the promotion and expansion of this new "law of comparative advantage". However, the fact is; it is enterprises that engage in trade, not countries and this simple fact is still waiting to be "**re-discovered**".

In conclusion; there is an essentially important law which affects the exchange relationships of products "between enterprises", i.e., the "**law of absolute advantage**". It applies not only to price but also to quality and design.

As to the question whether it is enterprises or countries that engage in trade one can simply state that; trade between countries is undertaken by individual enterprises but the data on the results of this trade or the "trade figures" are announced in the countries' trade balance report. Countries can always influence the size, nature, price, quality and direction of trade by imposing "country specific" trade policies. However, influencing trade is one thing and actually executing trade is another thing entirely. Failure to see this basic distinction has misled many economists and has impeded the development of further, realistic trade theories.

Based on what has already been discussed, we can conclude that the prospects of getting any sound insights from the Western trade theories are bleak. Western trade theories seem far away from comprehending or explaining actual trade relationships. In addition, they seem to fall short of any expectation of finding realistic and rational remedies for the present global economic problems and market deficiencies in today's international relationships. These factors make the Western trade theories a poor and unreliable source of inspiration.

This criticism of Western trade theories rules out the second option i.e., the development and application of Western theories of trade after a process of adaptation and adjustment to the Islamic principles. The underlying reason is the same; the inability of the Western trade theories to comprehend and explain actual trade relationships and their inadequacy in finding remedies to actual market deficiencies.

In short, the Western trade theories, generally, do not offer rational or realistic alternatives to the Islamic economists.

Adapting Secular Theories

Assume for a moment that the Western theories did contain the "desired" rationale as well as realistic ideas on trade; is it likely that they would be acknowledged and applied in analyses by the Islamic economists? It appears that a large number of Islamic economists who think like Chapra, who categorically refuses any "secular" ideas, would not welcome these ideas. Chapra's standpoint is very clear. He claims that there are economists: "**... who are trying to inject secularism into economics but they are bound not to succeed**." (Chapra; in Kahf (Ed); 1998; 122). Thus, according to Chapra and the Islamic economists who share his point of view, these so called "secular" Western principles can never be a sound source for them to base an economic model on.

Furthermore, if Chapra is correct then there is a very little chance that the secular economists of the West will ever accept any genuine Islamic economic theories either. That means unless they leave their secular ideas aside and convert to Islam. That is because; Western economists seem to consider their secular theories as irrevocable as the Islamic principles are for Islamic economists. Chapra's standpoint means that Islamic economics and Western secular economics have very few basic principles in common. In other words, regardless of how "universal" or "rational" Islamic trade theories are, they would not have much chance of being acknowledged in the Western secular economies. That is of course, as long as they prefer to remain secular and refuse to accept Islamic principles.

Developing an Islamic Trade Theory

In the light of previous arguments, since Islam is a universal religion, and the Western secular theories are unacceptable "for some", the rational thing to expect from them would be that they (Islamic economists, including the Islamic jurists) should do their utmost to develop a valid and universally applicable Islamic economic theory.

Based on the teachings of the Quran and the Sunnah, we can with confidence state that trading activities are welcome and even blessed by Islam. The experience so far shows that Islam is, in fact, in favor of "free-trade" among nations. According to Siddiqi, Islam not only favors freedom of trade but also freedom of mobility, i.e. man can go where he wants to trade. (see Siddiqi; in Ahmad (Eds.); 1992; 31). But he does not attempt, like many other Islamic economists, to explain the benefits gained from free trade and the free circulation of laborers in non-Muslim economies. If Siddiqi's message on free trade and free circulation is meant for Islamic countries only, then there may not be a need for any trade theory at all. All the Islamic tradesmen have to do is follow the principles laid down by Islam. The Islamic principles would guide Muslims behavior in conformity with Islamic values.

But if there is a message to the non-Islamic tradesmen and nations on the advantages of free-trade, then there should be a valid and universally applicable "scientific model" which explains the trade advantages to be gained from an "Islamic" point of view.

Below is a summary of the Islamic rules governing the economic transactions, of individuals, enterprises and nations that must be free from the following non-Islamic practices.

1. *"Riba i.e. interest on loans and exchange of unequal quantities of similar fungibles. Gold or silver or a particular paper currency must be exchanged in equal quantities. When gold and silver or different paper currencies are exchanged for one another, the quantities can be unequal but the exchange must be simultaneous.*
2. *Qimar i.e. gambling, bet and wager. The essence of gambling is taking a risk deliberately created or invited, which is not necessary to economic activity, to gain thereby.*
3. *Ghaban i.e. fraud, especially that relating to the characteristics of a product.*
4. *Ikrah i.e. coercion, or, imposing a contract, or a condition therein, on an unwilling party.*
5. *Bay' al mudtar i.e. exploitation of need e.g. by charging an exorbitantly high price.*
6. *Ihtikar i.e. withholding supplies of essential goods and services with a view to raising prices.*
7. *Najsh i.e. raising prices by making false bids.*

8. *Gharar i.e. hazard or uncertainty surrounding a commodity, its quantity, price, time of payment, time of delivery, etc. (with the provision that some little gharar can be ignored if it is humanly impossible to eliminate it).*
9. *Jahl mufdi ila al niza' i.e. such vagueness about commodity, its quantity, price, etc. as cannot be removed and may lead to dispute." (Siddiqi; in Ahmed, Eds.; 1992; 17).*

In fact, most of the items stated above which Siddiqi describes as "Islamic rules" are not unfamiliar to the non-Muslim world. As the matter of fact, many Western economies have, more or less, similar measures or policies on business transactions, especially regarding the items from 2 to 9.

In a paper where Siddiqi discusses the Islamic view on international trade, he states:

> *"The objective of international economic policies of Islamic nations should be a just and equitable world order most conducive to the choice by individuals and nations of the way of living willed by Allah, which would ensure for them success in this life as well as in the hereafter." (Siddiqi; in Ahmed Eds.; 1992; 10).*

It is highly likely that no Western or secular or non-Muslim community would object to a "**just and equitable**" world order, even without converting to Islam. There are many ethical values and principles which are essentially the same and shared by both Islamic and non-Islamic nations. Would it not be both logical and rational to take further steps from here and try to find more common ground and develop new economic models applicable to both Islamic and non-Islamic nations based on these common values and principles?

Well, maybe it is easier said than done. Siddiqi and other likeminded Islamic economists, state clearly that trade must be in conformity with the principles of Islam. Apparently developing new theories based on shared values do not seem an interesting option for them. But, as we know from experience and commonsense, being honest and reliable in economic activities and displaying altruistic behavior, among other things, are not characteristics specific to Muslims, only.

Ahmad, another Islamic scholar, argues in a paper entitled "The New International Economic Order", that there is a need for a new international economic order. He argues: "**Muslim people are, by and large, as dissatisfied with the prevailing international economic order as the people of the Third World in general**". (Ahmed; in Ahmed Eds.; 1992; 79). What he actually has in mind is an economic system based on the principles of the "**Shari'ah**." But he does not present any argument what the benefits to non-Islamic countries or non-Muslim tradesmen would be if they complied with the Shari'ah. He, too, seems to overlook or ignore the advantages of developing a new trade theory based on common values and principles shared by both the Muslim and non-Muslim communities alike.

To summarize; as far we know it looks like that an entirely new, alternative and universally applicable Islamic trade theory is nowhere in sight. And again, as far as we know, there seems to be no attempt to develop a trade theory based on common ethical values and principles either. The road to get there seems to be long and formidable; but a "coming of age" does not seem beyond reach.

In the next section, a bold attempt will be made to make a contribution to the development of a new theory of trade addressing both Islamic and non-Islamic countries. The arguments, hopefully, will to a large extent be in conformity, with the basic values and principles valid for both the Islamic and non-Islamic communities. No claim of universality is made, nor is there any claim to lay down "the" foundation stone of a new theory. The sole purpose is to make a humble contribution. However, the assumptions and the analyses aimed at explaining actual trade relations are claimed to be more realistic than those presented by the mainstream economists.

Some Remarks On Global Trade[12]

"While the comparative cost concept and other basic concepts have rarely failed to provide some help, they have usually carried the analyst only a little way toward adequate understanding."

Vernon; 1966; 190

Global? or International?

The purpose of this section is to present some views to contribute to the development of a new "alternative trade theory". The title might give the impression, at first glance, that two different trade types were to be discussed. The simple reason behind this misconception is the play on words which leads people to assume that "global trade" and "international trade" are two different types of trade. It should not come as a surprise to encounter a third word implying the same thing; "world trade". Yet, the fact is there is no difference at all in regard to substance.

Since the subject matter is economics, we will be discussing "**global**" or "**world**" or synonymously "**international**" trade and we shall use these terms interchangeably. Therefore, it would be misleading to use these concepts as if they are substantially different. Global trade refers to the export and import of products taking place on our planet not only "within" but also "among" the economic agents. Long before the use of the concept "global" in economic jargon enterprises were engaged in international or, synonymously global trade. In other words, "international" trade refers exactly to the same economic transactions that are found in "global" trade transactions. The interesting question is; why was the concept of globalization introduced as if basically different economic transactions were taking place, suggesting that world economic relations were undergoing a substantial change?

The answer is simple; Anglo-Saxon ideologists have a tendency to give a new name to an old town, as the Turkish idiom says, "unwelcome innovations are rarely well received[13]". For example, countries were labeled as "**developed**" and "**undeveloped**", for many years. Understandably this was not happily accepted

12 This section is quoted partly from H. Gürak, "Heterodox Economics", 2012, Peter Lang Int. Publ.

13 The original version of the Turkish idiom is: "Eski köye yeni adet getirmek".

by the countries which were labeled as "**undeveloped**". The term was perceived as abusive. Then, the term was replaced by "**developed and developing**" which seemed less abusive than the former. For a while the term "**digital-divide**" was introduced which did became somewhat popular. Soon after, a new and less objectionable term was introduced to please the relatively better-off developing countries; "**emerging**" countries.

The relevant critical question is; has anything substantially changed in regard to the global income disparities or the widening global gap? Still, a larger share, about 80 percent, of the world's population is relatively poor while a minority of about 20 percent enjoys a much higher standard of living. Changing the concepts has not been able to change inter-country inequalities and global poverty.

The main purpose of this section is to focus analysis on global trade relations.

Global Trade & Competition

Let us begin this section by asking a critical question: Do we really have access to a global market where all enterprises compete under the same "fair" conditions?

In order to have "fair" global competitive conditions, all enterprises from all countries should have, more or less, the same or similar technologies, e.g., production methods as well as access to a labor-force endowed with the same or similar qualities for similar products. Yet, we know very well from our observations that enterprises around the globe are not endowed with similar competitive qualities. There are enormous gaps between technological structures, financial facilities, institutional efficiencies and labor-force qualities of the developed and the developing countries and their enterprises. And this global situation tends to deteriorate, unless the existing data deceives us.

The most significant difference between the developed and developing countries is the difference between the qualities of the labor-forces. Taking measures to improve the quality of the labor-force is, primarily, a matter for the local rulers, and decision-makers. With appropriate and efficient programs in basic education problems such as increasing the rate of literacy or improving general education facilities can be easily achieved. However, improving the education or training infrastructure in developing countries to endow the labor-force with the necessary skills to efficiently use contemporary technologies, as found in the developed countries, requires a lot of time and effort, as well as the ability to establish the appropriate institutions and financial infrastructure. In the absence of a labor-force endowed with contemporary skills, it is practically impossible to use modern advanced technologies efficiently and supply products that are compatible in all the global markets. Eliminating, or at least reducing, global disparities in the skills of the labor-force should be given top priority.

Assume that all the disparities in the skills of the labor-force were eliminated with the wave of a wand; then would it be possible to have fair global competitive conditions amongst enterprises?

Given the present global economic circumstances and the structure of global institutions and their control by developed nations, it would be highly unlikely to find many high technology products and globally competitive enterprises originating from the developing countries which own and control the technology, although there might be some exceptions. The underlying reasons for this are present global economic circumstances and the imperfections encountered in technology markets. Enterprises from the developed countries, possessing high technology and operating globally, would not welcome any attempts to share their own "patented knowledge", e.g., technology, with "independent" enterprises from the developing countries (for a more detailed analysis see the Chapter on "Hidden Costs" in H. Gürak; 2012).

In order to have independent and global competitive strength, the enterprises in a developing country might pursue a policy to develop their own technologies and own their patent rights themselves, which would provide them with a greater flexibility to make their own decisions. As we know, Japan and South Korea had implemented a similar technology and science policy in the past. However, this is a costly and risky process. It is not simply sufficient to have a high quality labor-force that makes efficient use of the present technology. There would be a great need for "creative mental labor" along with an appropriate technological infrastructure, institutions and financial facilities. Assume, for a moment, that all these conditions are met; who can guarantee success in a global competitive market when confronted with giant and well experienced enterprises. Besides, it would be difficult to defend a technology policy to "re-invent" the already produced technologies which are presently in the hands of developed countries' giant enterprises. In a way, it would be like trying to re-invent the wheel; a useless waste of time.

Given the global economic circumstances in regard to the imperfections found in the technology market and the ability of the developing countries' enterprises to change all these, the so called development experts from global economic institutions and the developed countries, strongly advise the transfer of technology from the developing countries by the elimination of all barriers and encouraging foreign direct investments (FDIs). We can clearly see that the number of countries with generous FDI incentives is increasing constantly.

Global Competition & FDIs

Let us evaluate global competition from the point of view of the **FDI**s and global production. As indicated before, increasingly more developing countries are pursuing increasingly more liberal and generous economic policies in favor of **FDI**s which they hope will contribute to their economic growth rate. Yet, global income and wealth disparities seem to widen in time, instead of diminishing.

The crucial related question is; what happens to global competitiveness? Does it show a tendency to increase over time?

Unfortunately, it is impossible to give a positive answer? It is true that the number of laborers endowed with improved abilities is expanding, but that does not mean global competitiveness is increasing. To give an example, let us take a look at the automotive sector in Turkey again. As we know, Turkey has a large automotive sector with a substantial amount of exports to the global markets. Yet, there is no automobile producing enterprise owned and controlled by Turkish citizens with a Turkish trade-mark or own technology patent. The cars produced by brand names such as Fiat, Renault, Hyundai and Toyota are actually owned by the **GEs** of developed nations which also control both global production and distribution units. Their production plants in Turkey operate only as "**subcontractors**" and have no say in regard to crucial issues regarding the type of automobile, quantities produced and exported, etc. These critical decisions are made in the headquarters of the **GEs** with respect to their global interests. Irmiş (2008) describes position as;

> *"... a completely hierarchic vertical organization with developed country enterprises on the top placing of orders and subjacent developing country enterprises looking forward to carry out orders at predetermined prices." (Irmiş; 2008; 4-5).*

Given the nature of the subcontracting system, the huge financial, organizational and technological gap between the developed and developing country enterprises is bound to produce serious problems. One of the forth coming problems is pointed out by Irmiş (2008):

> *"This weakness and isolation of developing country enterprises against developed country enterprises is subject to exploitation by developed country enterprises, especially in "cost-reducing." (Irmiş; 2008; 5).*

For instance, assume that the concessions granted by the Turkish government are considered insufficient or unsatisfactory compared to another country's more generous concessions, or that the "real" wage-level in Turkey rises above "acceptable" limits, then subcontracted production can be moved partly or wholly to a country best serving the **GE**'s' global interests.

Is it logical and rational to refer to a system based on low-wage utilization as promoting global competition? A positive answer to this question seems unlikely. For example, it is true that the nature of global competition is changing in regard to automobile production. The productions of low-technology components are located in relatively lower-cost countries which promote **FDIs** with generous policies. Would it be rational to say that global competition in automobile sector is growing?

In order to say that global competition is growing, the number of independent profit making automobile producers has to increase. Under the circumstances described, the subcontracting of production does not seem to make any positive contribution to increased global competition. What the system does is the struggle to reduce cost which helps to increase global profits.

FDIs & Global Intra-Firm trade (IFT)

According to the conventional textbooks, foreign trade theories study, in general, the exchange relationships between two "countries" producing two-products, based on the law of comparative advantage. Yet a constantly growing amount of global trade is taking place intra-firm (**IFT**) that is among the enterprises scattered around the world belonging to the same headquarters. Intra-firm trade refers to exchange transactions among enterprises which belong partly or wholly to, in general, one globally operating enterprise (**GE**).

The **IFT** transactions can be divided into two categories:

1. **Production oriented IFT**: the trade of the products used in production, such as raw materials, machinery, tools, intermediaries, etc., between the parent-firm and the subsidiary or between subsidiaries.
2. **Distribution oriented**: the distribution of products produced by the parent-firm or a subsidiary in another country.

Our emphasis will cover trade between, for example, an automobile manufacturing unit in Turkey and the company's sales agent in Rome, or trade between the intermediary-goods supplying subsidiary and the final-product producing parent-firm or another subsidiary.

The Table: 2 provides some data on the size and extent of **IFT** on US economy. According to OECD data, the share of exports from US-based parent-firms to their subsidiaries of total exports reached to 32.1 percent and the imports to 46.7 percent of total imports.

Table: 3 shows data on intra-firm trade with a partner region. Just as in the case of the US enterprises, intra-firm trade displays rapid and steady growth.

According to data for 1999, **IFTs** account for about 14.8 percent of imports and 28.6 percent of exports. Table: 4 shows the dimensions of **IFTs** in some dynamic sectors. The main cause of rapid expansion of **IFTs** seems to be the restructuring of global production and distribution methods through the global operations of the **GEs** in accordance with their global interests.

Table: 2 Intra-firm trade of the US, with selected trading partners (As percent of all goods trade with partner country)

Imports	**Level 1999**	**Change 1992-1999**
Japan	73.7	-1.3
Mexico	66.4	3.1
Korea	49.3	22.5
Canada	43.1	-2.9
Eastern Europe	32.1	20.1
Taiwan	20.8	4.9
China	17.6	7.1
Total	46.7	1.7
Exports		
Mexico	44.3	5.6
Canada	42.4	-2.9
Japan	36.3	0.1
Taiwan	16.0	6.0
Eastern Europe	12.3	2.6
China	11.6	5.0
Total	32.1	1.2

Note: Partner countries shown are those with the highest level of intra-firm trade in 1999 or the largest increase over the period 1992-99.
Source: US Department of Commerce, 2001: in: OECD, 2008, VI. Intra-Industry & Intra-Firm Trade & the Int. of Prod., p.165, Tablo:VI.4

Table: 3 Intra-firm trade of Japan, where parent company is Japanese, with main trading blocs (As percent of all goods trade with partner region)

Exports	**1990**	**1999**	**Change in %**
Total	14.5	28.6	14.1
Rest of Asia	10.1	22.4	12.3
North America	20.9	36.8	15.8
Europe	12.0	29.0	17.0

Imports			
Total	4.2	14.8	10.6
Rest of Asia	6.3	22.5	16.1
North America	3.1	6.8	3.7
Europe	1.1	3.9	2.9

Source: Japanese Ministry of Economy, Trade and Industry: in: OECD, 2008, VI. Intra-Industry & Intra-Firm Trade & the Int. of Prod., s.165, Table: VI.3

Table: 4 US trade in products with a high degree of intra-firm trade (Percent)

	Share of total imports: exports	**Intra-firm trade**
Imports		
Transportation equipment	17.7	75.6
Computer & electronic products	20.8	66.3
Chemicals	6.4	59.3
Machinery except electrical	6.6	50.3
Electrical equipment, appliances & components	3.3	50.0
Exports		
Transportation equipment	15.6	41.2
Plastics & rubber products	2.2	40.7
Chemicals	9.9	39.3
Computer & electronic products	20.7	36.9
Electrical equipment, appliances & components	3.3	35.1

Source: US Department of Commerce, 2001: in: OECD, 2008, VI. Intra-Industry & Intra-Firm Trade & the Int. of Prod., p.166, Table: VI.5

Motives for IFT

The driving force behind **IFT** is the maximization of the global profits of the **GEs**. As well-known, nowadays practically all decision-makers in all countries are in a kind of race to attract more **FDIs** by various types of promotions including generous financial and other type of incentives. Not infrequently we observe that "**tax havens**" are created for the foreign investments of the **GEs** while quite often local producers complain about high taxes on locally supplied products.

Generous incentives along with the presence of relatively lower wage costs, attracts many **GEs** to move their production plants to developing countries in order to obtain mostly the low-technology and labor-intensive components required in production. Through this, they attempt to maximize global profits and gain a cost and/or price competitive advantage against their rivals. Even simply moving a plant site that requires cheap labor-services would be a sufficient incentive for a **FDI** and would lead to increase global profits, cet. par (Gürak; 2006-c).

Major Benefits of IFT

The major global benefits arising from the **IFT** of **GEs** can be classified, briefly, under five headings.

1. Increased productivity due to a global division of labor.
2. Starting the supply of products not produced before.
3. Increased employment.
4. Improved organizational and institutional skills.
5. Foreign currency earnings from exports, (if any).

Major Objections to IFT

There are many serious objections or criticisms to the global consequences of **IFT** practices which should not be neglected. Some of the criticisms are:

- Global production and trade is increasingly being shaped by **GEs** in accordance with their global interests, undermining the developing country interests.
- The underlying reason for the move of some production plants to developing countries is the opportunity to exploit a cheap labor-force.
- Many foreign enterprises do not, in fact, undertake any new investment which may add to productive capacity of the recipient country or creating new employment. Not they prefer to take-over the existing plants of production which simply means a change of ownership, not a real contribution to the productive capacity of the developing country.
- Practically, **IFT** does not make any significant contribution to technology transfer (discussed in Part-9).
- New global production relationships restructured by the **GEs** in accordance with their global interests do not indeed make any serious contribution to global competition. A given number of **GEs** continue their competition with

products supplied from plants scattered around the globe, but this does not mean global competition is increasing. In order for global competition to increase, the number of independent profit units has to increase, which is not the case regarding the **IFR** transactions.

- Due to the prevailing imperfections in technology markets, the trend does not indicate any signs of improving the technological and labor-force abilities of the enterprises in the developing countries. Under the present global circumstances, it seems highly unlikely for the developing countries and their enterprises to close the income, industrialization or the development gap.

IFT and the Ownership of Enterprises

Most of the **GEs** engaged in **IFT** originate from developed countries. Thus the global production and distribution is being shaped according to the interests of enterprises of these developed countries. At first glance, this may not seem problematic. However, when viewed from the point of view of global income distribution, it might well be a different matter. Let us review the situation in more detail. As we know, the national income of a country consists of wages and profits, including interest rate, which we called the "value added" (**VA**).

Assume that 25 percent of all the value added by foreign controlled enterprise is profit and this profit is transferred to the country designated by the headquarters which would quite likely be a developed country. This would imply a transfer of income from the developing to the developed country which would contribute to the income growth of the developed country while diminishing the developing country's share of global income.

We assumed that 25 percent was the officially declared profit rate realized. However, we also know that **GEs** have all the facilities and abilities to make clandestine income transfers from the developing to the developed parts of the world (see Gürak; 2003). Unfortunately, there is no way to estimate the exact amount of this income transfer through "official" channels. In fact, it is an implicitly accepted taboo to comment on the adverse effects of **FDIs**. The **GEs** with global interests do not welcome such criticism in regard to what really happens in the markets and do their utmost to prevent it. This can be considered as a natural reaction because of the amount of transferred income received by **DCs** via clandestine channels is known to be a huge amount when compared to the net income generated by the **FDI** in the host country. This would be subject to global debate and criticism. Therefore, the expectation that data on present day clandestine income transfers would be made public appears to be a highly unrealistic expectation. However, we can get a clear picture from the past data already published concerning these practices (Gürak, 1990). The On the other hand, in order to have a less unequal and less unfair world, we need more and accurate information about the channels and size of "unofficial" transfers and reliable data on the extent of it.

Global Trade & the Convergence of Wages & Prices

There is no doubt that global trade makes many positive contributions to national economies. For instance, under "fair" competitive conditions both individuals and national economies enjoying similar technological and institutional development levels would benefit highly from global trade in terms of price, quality and the variety of products, cet. par. The relevant and important question is what would the benefits of increased global trade be for all national economies in regard to the huge global disparities in income, technological and institutional infrastructure and competitive strength? Would it be a rational expectation for wages, prices and incomes to converge, under the present nature of global relationships?

According to some of the proponents of the neoclassical doctrine, provided the assumptions and the conditions of their theories are fulfilled, free global trade is expected to lead to the convergence of global wages and prices. Yet, the data and the experience gained from actual global transactions indicate that just the opposite is happening. As the barriers of global trade diminish, the income gap does not tend to close, but in reality becomes greater (Gürak, 2006). Besides, historical facts and experience tell quite a different story in regard to economic development, in contrast to the liberal trade policies advocated by the developed country institutions and the extension of these institutions; the international institutions.

Given the present nature of relationships, it is highly utopian to expect wages and prices to converge. The following seem to be major obstacles in achieving this goal:

1. The nature of global supply, distribution and technology transfer relationships.
2. Disparities between general development levels.
3. Disparities in labor-force qualities.
4. Global imperfections in technology markets.
5. Poverty.
6. Corruption and bad governance in the developing countries.

Instead of closing the global income and development gap, the present nature of global economic relationships tends to produce the following results.

- Wages and prices in the developed countries might converge or get closer.
- The global prices of industrial products in all countries might converge, but not the service sector prices, at least not in foreseeable future.
- The qualitative differences of consumer products might diminish or even disappear completely in both, developed and developing countries; but the quantity of per capita consumption is unlikely to converge.
- It seems like a purely utopian expectation for the developed and the developing countries' wage-level to converge, at least under the present global economic conditions.

Concluding Remarks

Let us present the major findings briefly:

- There seems to be no significant difference in the nature of the trade relationships between national enterprises in the domestic markets or between enterprises at a global level, given "fair" and equally competitive conditions and regulations for all the enterprises concerned. Naturally, there should be neither any enterprise with a monopolistic or oligopolistic power in the markets nor any visible or invisible barriers to trade.
- Global economic trends show that trade barriers hampering global trade in industrial goods are diminishing progressively.
- Elimination of all trade barriers among countries with the same or similar development levels would make a positive contribution to global trade.
- Elimination of all trade barriers among countries with the same or similar development levels would contribute to the maximizing of consumer benefits.
- Protection of the "infant" sectors for a pre-determined time-period is highly likely to make a positive contribution to global trade and to global economic growth. Because, infant sector enterprises mature over time as global competition increases due to the participation of more competitors in the global market which also would affect consumers in positive way.
- Enterprises lagging behind in contemporary level of technological advancement cannot survive the long-term challenge of their rivals in competitive markets. Therefore, all competitive enterprises have to strive to keep up with the technological changes. However, as indicated in Section-7, there are serious imperfections in the global technology markets to the detriment of the "technological" late-comers. The present nature of the technology markets, the consequent global economic relationships, together with historical developments, does not seem to make a positive contribution to global competition.

For instance, scattering the automobile production plants around the globe by using the wholly or partly owned subsidiaries of a "given number" of Globally Operating Enterprises would not really increase global competition. To increase global competition, the number of independent automobile producers who seek to maximize their profit margins has to increase. To overcome this obstacle, the imperfections in the technology markets have to be eliminated or, at least, the transfer conditions of technology have to improve in favor of the developing countries' enterprises.

- The share and significance of intra-firm trade (**IFT**) has been constantly growing. In principle, growing global trade is a good sign responsible for global economic growth. However, it is also liable to lead to some undesirable economic consequences, especially in the more "**clandestine income transfers**". For example, assume that a foreign-owned enterprise-"A" undertakes an investment in Turkey to produce automobiles. Further assume that some of the inputs used in the supply of the automobiles are imported from a source and at a price determined by the parent enterprise. The inputs imported may be available in the global markets at global competitive prices. But, although the global prices for the imported inputs might be much lower, the plant in Turkey has no choice but to purchase these inputs from the parent company's sources and at a price pre-determined by headquarters, in accordance with the global interests of the parent enterprise. This decision from "headquarters" may result in, or may be used for, a "**disguised transfer of profits**" to a pre-determined source, in accordance with its global profit policy.
- The global interests of enterprises engaged in **IFT** are more important for the foreign-owner than the potential benefits or damages to the host-country's economy, and not infrequently, these interests are incompatible.
- **IFT** transactions may lead to the economic dependency of the host-country's economy on the foreign global enterprise, e.g., the **GE**.

When developing a "new" theory of trade one should genuinely take into consideration the "**global benefits**" to all countries. That means these benefits should not be evaluated only from the perspective of developed country enterprises as it is the case today. In addition, the defects in the present technology market should be eliminated and access to technology should be easy and egalitarian for all enterprises. There ought to be no monopoly on the patent of a "new" technology by one enterprise only. To serve this purpose, technology producing units can be organized as "**globally independent profit units**" without any organic ties to any specific enterprise and be prepared to license the patented technology to all enterprises at a global market price without any discrimination.

Chapter-6

Islam & Interest
From the perspective of an economist

Introduction

The concept "interest" or "riba" for some has been one of the most vehemently debated subjects in economics; probably "the" most vehemently debated one. The notion of interest and its implications were known long before the advent of Islam. Babylon had developed a loan system in the second Millennium BC, as early as 1760 BC, where some restrictions on interest payment were imposed by the code of Hammurabi, a code of Babylonian law named after its author.

> *"The Code of Hammurabi indicates a 20-percent interest rate on money and grain, and it stipulates that a merchant charging a higher rate would forfeit the amount lent. By contrast God's law to Israel prohibited making loans on interest to needy fellow Israelites." (http-16)*

In spite of all the criticism, the payment of interest has been practiced in various forms all around the world, even in Muslim countries. Today, it is a common and routine practice in the non-Muslim world. Though getting interest is not permitted in the religion of Islam, Muslims are not unfamiliar with the system. For example, oil income rich Muslim rulers and their close associates keep their financial assets worth billions of US Dollars in the Western financial system. Nobody is naive enough to believe that they do not get any interest on these assets.

On the one hand, there is the Islamic rule forbidding interest payment, and on the other, the Western economic system which considers the payment of interest as a natural function of the system. According to Islam, getting or paying any interest is "haram", e.g. forbidden under religious law. Fettullah Gülen says: "**The Islamic ruling on this issue is definite and clear. '...** ***Allah hath permitted trade and forbidden usury'***. (Baqara; 2-275)" (Gülen; 2013).

This is a serious issue for those who get interest, says Gülen, because:

> *"Those who devour usury behave as Satan demands and desires, as if driven to madness by his touch. They are as like the shadows of Satan on the ground. As devouring usury shrivels them up, and they constantly enter into speculative transactions. They forestall the market and lie. [...] They can sacrifice religion, devoutness and all kinds of sacral for the sake of interest." (Gülen; 2013).*

Gülen's view on one specific aspect seems in need of further clarification. When he says that **the societies, in which interest is free, are always precarious**, does Gülen refer to the economic crises which are the chronic failures of capitalism? Or does he mean that those who get interest will be **precarious in the life hereafter**?

Evaluating the interest from a sociological point of view, Gülen suggests that the Muslims should be cautious.

"While interest makes the rich even richer, it makes the poor even poorer. Thus, the gap between the two classes widens as the time passes. In the end, all bridges between them collapses and these two classes become the fierce enemies of each other.

There would be tyranny, molestation and despotism from top to bottom. The attitude of antagonism, hatred and particular malice would grow from bottom to top. The society which would enter into a big chaos would someday totally perish from the social geography." (Gülen; 2013).

The main purpose of this study is to evaluate the Islamic principles governing the "interest issue" from the scientific perspective of an economist. The primary and the principle source will be the Holy Book of the Koran. The secondary source will be the Sunnahs, "**the sayings and practices**" of the Prophet Mohammad.

The Koran refers to the issue of "interest" in four Verses. The Verse "Baqara" clearly mentions the term "**loan interest**" and strictly prohibits any "**surplus**" or "**excessive payment**" on the initial amount of the loan. Naturally, since the Holy Book is not an economics textbook, there is no definition or scope or criterion of the term "interest".

In addition to confirming the prohibition of "loan interest", the Prophet emphasizes another type of interest; the "**commodity interest**". Therefore, the study will cover two kinds of interest.

1. Loan interest.
2. Commodity interest.

When Islam was being revealed about 1,400 years ago, economic relationships within countries and between nations already existed, but no social science called "economics" as we know today. The economic transactions and related problems were fewer in kind and less complicated in nature than todays. Whenever Muslim tradesmen encountered any problem, they usually consulted the Islamic scholars, especially the lawyers (faqih) to find remedies consistent with Islamic principles. That is because at that time the Holy Book of the Koran dealt not only with ethics but was used as the guide for every aspect of life. If they could not find the solution in the Koran, then they searched the Sunnahs to find the appropriate answer to the problem. If neither Koran nor the Sunnahs pointed to a resolution, then they asked the Islamic scholars for a fetwa, i.e., a ruling consistent with Islamic principles. This tradition still goes on today, especially in the more conservative areas.

In addition to the conventional Islamic scholars a new group of people called "Islamic economists" has emerged in the last 60-70 years who are explaining, commenting and seeking solutions on economic matters. They try to present Islamic arguments on all economic issues ranging from trade to growth, employment, insurance and economic development. The most favored and frequently debated subject seems to the topic of "interest". Nowadays, there is a large pool of knowledge to be drawn from on the subject of interest as well as other related economic matters. We also will attempt to benefit from such accumulated knowledge on Islamic economics. However, we will not simply be content with these available and accumulated sources but we will go on to make a bold attempt to present some personal and somewhat "different" definitions, explanations and comments to the conventional ones from an economist's perspective. Certainly the utmost attempt will be made not to contradict any fundamental Islamic principles.

The courage to present new arguments is based upon the Islamic viewpoint in regard to scientific issues viz. Islam encourages scholarly thinking and learning. Reportedly, a Hadith, (a saying of the Prophet), states that "one should even go to China to learn". The meaning of the Hadith is better understood if one takes into account the travel and transportation conditions 1,400 years ago. It is our hope that the contemporary Islamic scholars will read and evaluate this work with the same type and degree of tolerance that was manifest 1,400 years ago even if they do not agree with its content.

What is Interest (or Riba)?

Since the subject of study is "interest" in Islam, it is imperative to define just what is meant by the term "interest", in order to avoid any misperception or misinterpretation in the ensuing arguments.

Some may claim that everything about the interest is already said and done and there's nothing "new" to add. However, we do not accept this point of view that is why we have undertaken this study. Islamic scholars who repeatedly quote the same Verses and Sunnahs about interest in their arguments seem to be seeking some kind of "divine support" for their arguments. But, can we comfortably state, from a "scientific perspective" that these quotations are sufficient and are a scientific and universally applicable explanation?

Since the divine rulings in the Holy Book of the Koran and the Sunnahs are not economic texts, we have to develop "human" economic scientific theories in order to comprehend "human" economic relationships. However in doing this it is essential not to demean or contradict in any way the tenets of the religion of Islam.

Some Views about Interest

According to the Islamic faith getting or paying interest or "riba" is prohibited. The substance of this prohibition is from the Verses of the Koran; the secondary source is the Sunnahs of the Prophet. Based on these sources, Islamic scholars attempt to explain the scope and implications of "riba" by presenting their subjective arguments whenever necessary. For example, according to the Department of Religious Affairs of Turkey (Diyanet)[14]:

> *"The Islamic term riba in the dictionary means 'to increase, to multiply, to heighten, to inflate, to expand', used as an unrequited "surplus", or in relation to trade of the same kind of reproducible Objects with future delivery, stated as a condition in the agreements. [...] It is permitted to trade different types of objects such as gold, silver and similar types or wheat, barley, date, salt and similar types, on the condition of prompt delivery. In similar fashion, a surplus in the trade of the dry date with the fresh date, the good quality date with the bad quality date, trade of silver in return of gold delivery in future; it is permitted to exchange gold for gold, silver for silver only for prompt delivery and in equal weights (Buhari, Büyü', 77-81; Müslim, Müsâkât, 79-85). [the] Koran prohibits, with a clear language, interest in the Era of Ignorance, loan interest (ribe'd-deyn) or commodity interest known as ribe'n-nesie," a surplus in return of future delivery, and [the] Sunnahs confirm this prohibition." (Diyanet-2).*

An Islamic web site, "Questions on Islam", describes interest (riba) as follows:

> *"Riba means redundancy, abundance and increase. Therefore, extra money or property charged in return for anything lent is included in the scope of prohibition. Riba also means haram (unlawful) earning. According to another definition in Islamic Law, "Interest is the redundancy conditioned in trade." (http-12).*

And it explains why riba is forbidden:

> *"There is nobody who does not know that interest is forbidden in Islam. The reason why interest is forbidden by divine order is obvious: It is forbidden because Allah forbade it. Just as fasting or giving alms is fard because of "divine order", so too is interest forbidden for the same reason." (http-12).60 saniye sonra oturumunuz kapatılacaktır. Veri kaybını engellemek için işleminizi kaydediniz.*

An "Ilmihâl[15]" prepared by the Diyanet explains why interest is prohibited as follows:

> *"Prohibition of interest is one of the fundamental principles of Islam. As stated before, in principal, Islam does not intervene in the human relations that do not cause any harm and injustice, legal or commercial life that follows a strait path; Islam only warns in case of improper or unjust practice, introduces some restrictions in this sense. Prohibition of interest is of this kind. (Diyanet-3).*

Although some Islamic scholars have somewhat dissident opinions on some of the "practices" involving interest, there is a general consensus on the "prohibition"

---

14 Diyanet: "Türkiye Diyanet İşleri Başkanlığı"; from now on, only "Diyanet".
15 Ilmihâl: The book written for the purpose to teach the principles of Islam.

of interest. One of the critical terms used in connection to interest is "**surplus**". The other critical term is "**unjust income**". The important question is; in what sense is there a "surplus" or an "unjust income"? For example, does the term refer to a surplus in terms of the labor-time employed? Or a surplus in terms of the risk assumed? Could it be a surplus accruing in exchange of objects or money? What is the criterion or criteria? The criterion of the "surplus" or "unjust income" needs to be explained in a rational and commonly acceptable manner. The critical key terms are "**surplus**", "**unjust income**" and "**criterion**".

Ashker-Wilson think there are two motives for the prohibition of interest; moral and economic:

> "The moral motive revolves on the principle of not exploiting the poor and the needy through charging them interest on borrowed money. The economic motive emanates from:
>
> 1. the principles of justice, which is deemed as the fairness of dividing both gains and losses between the parties concerned in business deals,
> 2. the encouragement of labor effort and the promotion of a positive contribution by capital owners to economic activities, and
> 3. alleviating the tendency for the concentration of wealth in the hands of the few. Islam is not against being rich, providing that, among other things, this is not achieved through idle and selfish activities such as the lending money for interest." (Ashker-Wilson; 2006).

Ashker-Wilson and many other Islamic scholars writing on interest normally do not bother to define interest relative to any specific criterion. It is considered as sufficient to quote some Verses or Hadiths on its prohibition. We, however, are highly interested in a comprehensive and "scientific" definition in relation to some form of criteria.

Below, interest will be studied under two headings:

1. **Loan interest.**
2. **Commodity interest.**

Let's see what our principal source, the Holy Book of the Koran, has to say on the subject, before considering the related views in the Sunnahs.

Interest as referred to in the Koran

According to Islam, borrowing is permissible. We know that even the Prophet himself used to borrow from time to time. What is not permissible is any "surplus" demanded on the loan advanced. As the matter of fact, borrowing can certainly be rewarding, especially if the debtor has no intention of default.

"Allah the Glorious helps those who get into debt with the intention of paying back later. A hadith narrated by Abu Huraira says: "Whoever gets into debt with the intention of paying back later, Allah enables him to pay it back. Whoever takes one's property with the aim of wasting it, Allah wastes him away and he cannot pay back." (Bukhari, Istiqrad 2). The importance of aim in getting into debt is clearer in the following hadith narrated by Abu Umamah: "If anyone takes other people's money with the intention of repaying it and then he or she should die without settling the debt, Allah will pay the debt on his behalf. And if anyone takes money or property (of others) with the intention of destroying it, Allah will destroy him." (Kamil Miras, Tajrid-i Sarih, 7/273)." (http-12).

The Quranic verse says:

"If the debtor is in a difficulty, grant him time till it is easy for him to repay. But if ye remit it by way of charity, that is best for you if ye only knew." (Baqara; 2:280).

However, a debtor, who does not pay back although he can afford to, is considered to be unjust to the creditor. The following is stated in a hadith:

"**It is injustice of one who is able to pay his debt to delay it**." *(Bukhari, Hawala 1, 2; Muslim, Musakat 33; Abu Dawud, Buyu 10; Tirmidhi, Buyu 68). (http-12).*

There are four Verses in the Koran specifically addressing the interest issue. They are, in accordance with the date of Revelation are; **The Romans**; 30/39, **Women;** 4/160-161, **The Family of Imrân;** 3/130, **Baqara;** 2/275-276-278. The first two Verses do not mention specifically any prohibition. The third commands: "**Devour not usury, doubled and multiplied; but fear Allah**." And finally in **Baqara** interest is prohibited with a clear statement.

The relevant and critical questions are; **does the Holy Book define interest, i.e., a surplus"? And does it name any criterion with which to measure this "surplus"?**

Let's see what the Verses say.

Koranic Verses on Interest (According to their Date of Revelation)

The first Verse on interest in "**The Romans**" was revealed in Mecca. Following the revelation of a related Verse, the Prophet had sent a letter to the Governor of Mecca, requiring the Amirs, who had a conflict about loaned money, to forgo the interest payment on the loan. The message to Amirs was clear: "**Either they accept that or declare war on them**." (Taberî, VI, 23 in Diyanet-4).

Here are the Verses:

1- The Romans

> **39**. *That which you give in usury for increase through the property of (other) people, will have no increase with Allah: but that which you give for charity, seeking the Countenance of Allah, (will increase): it is these who will get a recompense multiplied.*

There is no clear prohibition of interest in this Verse. However it states that it "… ***will have no increase with Allah***". What the Verse suggests is "**giving charity**" for the "**Countenance of Allah**". As we see, there is no definition of interest or any criteria how to measure the "surplus". Some scholars interpret the expression "… ***will have no increase with Allah***" as if it *implies* a prohibition, though some consider this perception as an exaggeration.

2- Women

> **160**. *For the iniquity of the Jews We made unlawful for them certain (foods) good and wholesome which had been lawful for them;- in that they hindered many from Allah's Way.*

> **161**. *That they took usury, though they were forbidden; and that they devoured men's substance wrongfully;- We have prepared for those among them who reject faith a grievous punishment..*

Verses 160 and 161 criticize the Jews for getting interest though they were forbidden to get any. But there is no prohibition for the Muslims, yet. A wider interpretation that includes the Muslims would be an exaggeration. As we see again, there is neither any definition of interest nor any criteria by which to measure the "surplus".

3- The Family of Imrân

> **130**. *O ye who believe! Devour not usury, doubled and multiplied; but fear Allah. that ye may (really) prosper.*

This is the first Verse that prohibits interest with a clear language about two-three years after the Hegira (the flight of the Prophet to Medina, circa 622 A.D.). The emphasis is on the "**doubled and multiplied usury**". The details of the "doubled and multiplied" are open to debate and in need of clarification. According to Islamic historians, in the Era of Ignorance before Islam, when the Arab debtor could not repay his debt with interest on time, the repay period was extended but an additional and often excessive amount was requested i.e. interest on the loan. That is, probably, the critical issue referred to in the Verse. However, we cannot define the type of interest at issue with any certainty. That is because; there is also interest to be paid at the end of the "initial" period of the loan which is also prohibited. It is not definite in the Surah which type of interest is meant; is it, the one for the "extended" period with additional interest payment or the interest paid for all periods, including the initial one.

Thereby we learn specifically that getting interest is prohibited for Muslims as well, but yet again there is still no definition of interest or any criteria dealing with how to measure the "surplus".

4 - Baqara

With the revelation of Baqara, we get detailed information on interest:

> **275.** *Those who devour usury will not stand except as stand one whom the Satan by his touch Hath driven to madness. That is because they say: "Trade is like usury," but Allah hath permitted trade and forbidden usury. Those who after receiving direction from their Lord, desist, shall be pardoned for the past; their case is for Allah (to judge); but those who repeat (the offense) are companions of the Fire: They will abide therein (forever).*
>
> **276.** *Allah will deprive usury of all blessing, but will give increase for deeds of charity: For He loveth not any ungrateful and wicked.*
>
> **278.** *O ye who believe! Fear Allah, and give up what remains of your demand for usury, if ye are indeed believers.*
>
> **279.** *If ye do it not, take notice of war from Allah and His Messenger. But if ye repent, ye shall have your capital sums: Deal not unjustly, and ye shall not be dealt with unjustly.*

The message is very clear and needs no interpretation: getting interest is forbidden. If getting interest is not avoided or abstained from, one would be considered "**at war with Allah and his Apostle Messenger**".

However, yet again, there still is no definition of interest or any criteria that can be used to measure the "surplus. On this matter, the Ilmihal prepared by Diyanet says:

> *[The] Koran refers to the prohibition of interest in various parts in different styles of wordings and expressions. But there is nowhere a definition of riba, its distinctive features and its scope." (Diyanet-3).*

To summarize; there are four Verses directly related to the issue of interest (riba) and the last two specifically forbids the getting of interest for Muslims. However, there is no definition of interest or any criteria how to measure the "surplus". As the matter of fact, this is quite natural; because the Koran is not a textbook of economics.

Getting even a tiny "surplus" (interest) is forbidden. The purpose is to avoid or abstain from getting any "**unjust income**". But, what is the definition of this "**unjust income**"**?** What are the criteria for "unjust-ness"? And **how can it be measured?**

An Hypothesis: Loan Interest

Assume that Mustafa lends 100 TL to Mehmet to buy two kilos of meat worth exactly 100 TL. The debtor repays 100 TL a year later. At first sight, there is no "surplus" or any "unjust income". But, could there be a "disguised" unjust situation?

Whether there is anything "unjust" depends on some details. Let's suppose that Mustafa who lent the 100 TL which bought two kilos of meat at the time, can now, after a year, purchase only one kilo of meat for 100TL. Is there an "unjust" outcome?

A. Bayındır tells a good and realistic story about just this situation;

> *"Somebody borrowed 450 TL in the year 1950 from my father which was not repaid until October 1999, the year this paper was written. At that date, the lowest amount of money was 10,000 TL and all one could buy with that money was a chewing gum. But, back in 1950, one could buy 75 grams of gold. That is because; one gram of 24 carat gold was worth six TL at that time. (Bayındır; 2009).*

Under the circumstances, can we say it was "just" to pay back only 450 TL? Who is subject to the "unjust" treatment? Would it not be better, from the Islamic point of view, to use the criterion of "purchasing power" to avoid "unjust-ness"?

Imam Ebu Yusuf's views support A. Bayındır.

> *"The majority of Islamic lawyers ignore the fluctuations in the purchasing power in case of cash money lending. However, Imam Ebû Yusuf takes these fluctuations in purchasing power of metal money into consideration the in the payment back, except for gold and silver. In case of a decline or increase in the purchasing power, back payment is worth equivalent to the value of gold or silver at the date of the sale agreement; if the debt arises from a loan (karz) agreement, the delivery date (kabz) is taken into account. Thereby Ebû Yusuf does not take the inflation variation in metal money into consideration. However, his approach does not include the debts arising from gold or silver money at his time. Ibn Âbidîn specifically emphasized that point. (Ibn Âbidîn, Reddül-Muhtâr, IV, 24, Resâil, II, 63, 64; Tenbîhu'r-Rukûd alâ Mesâili'n-Nukûd, Mecmuatu'r-Resâil, II, 52; el-Fetâ-vâl-Bezzâziye, (Hindiyye kenarında), c. IV, 510)." (http-13).*

Now, let's see what the Sunnahs have to say on the issue of interest.

Sunnahs and the Interest

We shall try to gain an insight into the concepts "surplus" and "unjust income" by reviewing the Sunnahs, (the sayings and practices of the Prophet), the secondary source of Islamic principles. This is the conventional practice every time Muslims encounter a problem for which there is no explanation in the principal source of Muslims; the Koran. According to Diyanet:

"The Sunnah of the Prophet explained the "prohibition of interest", showed its practice, in addition, qualified some practices as interest and prohibited them that were not pointed out in Koran.

For example, the Prophet ruled out in his Farewell Sermon: "Truly, the usury of the Era of Ignorance has been laid aside forever. Your capital, however, is yours to keep. You will neither inflict nor suffer any inequity." (Diyanet-3; http-12).

Let us remind ourselves of the 130th. Verse of the Sunnah entitled, "The Family of Imrân":

"O ye who believe! Devour not usury, doubled and multiplied; but fear Allah. that ye may (really) prosper."

And the Hadith stated above confirms this:

"Truly, the usury of the Era of Ignorance has been laid aside forever."

However, it is still not definite which type of interest is meant; i.e., the one for the "extended" period with additional interest payment, or, the interest paid for all periods, including the initial one.

Commodity Interest

The Holy Book of the Koran makes reference only to the "loan interest" but the Hadiths extend this prohibition by introducing "commodity interest". Regarding the Hadith interpretation, one of the reliable sources is the Ilmihal of the Diyanet which states:

"The Prophet had forbidden some practices and types of trade with the concern they would lead to interest or for they implied interest. For example, the well-known Hadith "eşyâ-yı sitte" or "emvâl-i ribeviyye" ruled: "Do not trade gold for gold, silver for silver, wheat for wheat, barley for barley, date for date, and salt for salt. There is an exception if they are in equal quantities and immediately paid. Whoever increases or get [a] surplus, he gets/pays interest. There is no difference between who gets and who gives." (Diyanet-3).

There is no doubt that the Diyanet makes reference to "commodity interest". Now we can discern two distinguishing details about the prohibition of interest. Interest occurs;

1. when a surplus, or an extra payment, is made in addition to the original amount of loan; "loan interest"; and/or,
2. when inequality in the immediate exchange of the same goods takes place; i.e., "commodity interest" which also includes "timed-payment" except for those cases concerning direct monetary payment.

As clearly indicated in the Ilmihal, trade of the "same objects" such as gold or silver or salt must be in "equal quantities" and "paid immediately". If any part of the trade attempts to get a surplus, it is considered "interest" and that is strictly forbidden by Islam.

Also the trade in dry dates for fresh dates or good quality dates for low quality dates is forbidden. The traded quantities and qualities must be equal and payment made immediately. There is well-known rumor related to the Prophet regarding the trading of dates:

> *"It is economic thought in the qur"àn and sunnah reported that the Prophet said to one of his companions, Bilal ibn Rabah, who exchanged two measures of low quality dates for one measure of high quality (dates), "It is exactly Riba. Never do it, but if you want to buy such (high quality) dates you can sell yours for money and then buy the dates you want" (flaoeioe Muslim). In addition to seeking the advantages of monetary transactions over the less advanced market mechanism of barter transactions, monetary transactions help eliminate the elements of ambiguity related to the process of estimating 'equivalence' in the objects traded. (Ashker-Wilson; 2006)."*

However, if the traded objects are "different", the "equal quantity" rule does not apply. The related Hadith says:

> *"On the condition that the objects are different and payment made immediately, trade anyway you desire. On the condition of immediate payment, gold for silver, silver for gold, wheat for date, barley for date can be traded." (Buhârî, "Büyû'", 77-81; Müslim, "Müsâkat", 79-85)." (Diyanet-3).*

In the Koran, there was no rule regarding the trading of "the same object" in "equal quantities" for "immediate payment". Now this rule exists. The traded objects may be "different" in nature but payment must be immediate. The prophet; "**... permitted trade of different objects on the condition of immediate payment.**" (Diyanet-3). The condition of the equality of quantities does not apply when objects are different.

Another matter not specifically ruled on in the Koran is trading using a timed-payment.

> *"The only kind of timed-payment transaction permitted by Islam is the one where money is used in payment. When money is used in this type of transaction, the trade is permitted regardless of whether the commodity is delivered immediately and money paid at a later time or money paid immediately and commodity delivered at a later time." (Diyanet-4).*

The rationale behind the above restrictions seems to lie in discouraging barter transactions in favor of monetary transaction." (Ashker-Wilson; 2006). The purpose seems to avoid the emergence of any "unjust income" in commodity trade.

As we have seen, "the same objects" can be traded in equal quantities for immediate payment. However, there may be some exceptions. We have already learned of the Prophet's prohibition of the practice of trading fresh dates for dry dates.

> *"However, upon the needs and requests of garden owners in Medina, the Prophet permitted the garden owners to trade the fresh date on [the] tree for the equivalent amount of dry dates (bey'u'l-arâyâ, bey'u'l-ariyye) by appraisement. However, considering the probability of the date on tree to be in excess, the surplus will be interest. But, upon a specific need, the Prophet permitted it as an exceptional case. [...] Responding to the needs of garden owners or the dry date owners who wish to eat fresh dates, the Prophet is said to permit this small scale trade on the ground it would not lead to interest, exploitation and deception." (Diyanet-3).*

To summarize; now we have detailed information on the commodity trade and can conclude that:

1. In commodity trade, payment should be immediate.
2. The timed-payment of commodities should be avoided except for cases where "money" is used in the transaction.
3. The trade of "the same objects" should be in "equal quantities".

However, we still lack a definition of interest based on the criterion of "unjustness". As the Ilmihal clearly states:

> *"There is no definition of riba (interest) in the Koran or in the Sunnahs; but merely some pronounced examples." (Diyanet-3).*

Interest According to the "Islamic Encyclopaedia"

"Islamic Encyclopaedia" describes the features of riba as:

> *"... a technical term, usury and interest, and in general any unjustified increase of capital for which no compensation is given. Derivatives from the same root are used in other Semitic languages to describe interest. A. In classical Islamic law. 1. Transactions with a fixed time limit and payment of interest, as well as speculations of all kinds, formed an essential element in the highly developed trading system of Mecca." (http-11).*

The key concept is any "**unjustified increase**" or as we say "**surplus**". But the cause or the source of this "**unjustified increase**" and the criterion on which this increase is based is not explained. Why is interest forbidden in Islam?

> *"There is nobody who does not know that interest is forbidden in Islam. The reason why interest is forbidden by divine order is obvious: It is forbidden because Allah forbade it. Just as fasting or giving alms is fard because of "divine order", so too is interest forbidden for the same reason. It is the only reason why we worship. Besides, there are some other*

reasons following the divine order. It is quite normal because, the One who ordered it knows very well the true nature and disposition of everything and how everything is supposed to be." (http-12).

In short, avoiding giving and taking interest is a requirement of serving Allah.

According to Diyanet's Islamic Encyclopedia, one of the reasons of the prohibition of interest is related to production. It is claimed that interest payment prevents the full-capacity utilization of resources. That is because; the cost of the interest payment is claimed to raise the cost of production and thereby the price of the commodities. Interest payment is also believed to cause "injustice" in the case of consumption loans. Therefore, the prohibition of interest is justified.

Three Types of Interest

According to the "Encyclopaedia of Islam", there are three types of loan interest which are not mentioned in the Koran or the Sunnahs.

1. Negative interest.
2. Inflation interest.
3. Discount interest.

1. "Negative" interest

Normally, nominal interest rates at banks or similar kinds of establishments are positive. However, when the nominal rate is below the inflation rate, the "real" interest rate will be "negative". The "Islamic Encyclopedia" of the Diyanet has a similar definition:

"Regarding a loan agreement with interest, if fewer amounts of commodities and services are purchased with the loaned money plus the interest, at the end of the term of loan, the interest is negative. Negative interest occurs when the interest rate is below the inflation rate." (Diyanet-4).

The question is whether negative interest should be forbidden just like positive interest. The answer is: "… **the negative interest should be subject to the same ruling as the positive interest**." (Diyanet-4). That is because; the reason behind the prohibition of interest is the injustice which applies to both cases equally, says Diyanet's Islamic Encyclopeadia. No distinction is made between negative and positive interest; "**injustice**" occurs in both cases. But, what is the criterion for "injustice"?

2. "*Inflation*" *and Interest*

As we know, inflation means an increase in the general price level, while deflation means a fall in the general price level. According to the Islamic Encyclopedia:

> *"It is not correct to justify the interest payment by establishing a correlation between inflation and interest. Whether the interest rate is above or under or equal to the inflation rate, it does not eliminate the injustice caused by the interest." (Diyanet-4).*

Let's consider a transaction in terms of loan money and assume that debtor gets 100 TL for a certain period. Further assume that the price inflation rate is 10 percent during the same period of loan. If the debtor repays 100 TL only, the loan giver will suffer a loss in purchasing power. That is because; he no longer can get the same objects in the same quantities for the same price. While there is a "negative inflation" for the lender, the debtor benefits from the transaction. Would it be unfair to/ call the benefit accruing to the debtor "**unjust**"?

As quoted before, the "Islamic Encyclopedia" of Diyanet rules that neither negative nor positive interest should be collected; both are "not permissible". That is because; just like a surplus in favor of one side is considered as interest, a decline accruing to the other side is also considered as interest. But, in another sentence, the "Islamic Encyclopedia" presents another ruling where receiving interest equal to the inflation rate is "permissible".

> *"The Islamic judicial reasoning in conjunction with maintaining stability, explicitness and justice is a requirement of the Islamic principle with regard to compensation in the case of a decline in the purchasing power of money due to inflation, especially to protect the value of money against inflation in loans and to develop measures to realize that goal. (Diyanet-4).*

If a surplus or an addition equal to the inflation rate is not "unjust", then it should not be called "interest". That is because; "any kind of interest" is forbidden in Islam. It would be better if it were called something else.

3. "*Discount*" *Interest*

Discount implies a "reduction"; it can be a reduction in the price of an object or a reduction in the amount of a loan. In this case, "discount interest" refers to the latter. What Islam specifically considers as "discount interest" is explained in the following quotation:

> *"A unique loan situation where an interest rate is determined, and then that percentage is removed from the loan amount, and the borrower is given the remainder of the loan." (http-12).*

"Discount interest" is forbidden because it is like an interest on a time based loan which increases by the amount of interest.

> *"It is indisputable that either the lender or the borrower will be treated unfairly when interest is charged on lending." (http-12).*

Thus, "unjustness" occurs in transactions involving discount interest?

Now we have information about the three "new" types of inflation as specified in the Islamic Encyclopedia. But, there is still no consensus on the nature, extension and types of the interest.

"Other" Views on Interest

As stated before, the Islamic scholars, in general, agree that any kind of interest is forbidden. However, there are some dissidents. On the interest question, Hasan says:

> *"Muslim scholars agree, with few dissentions, that in Islam the prohibition of* riba *is total and complete. The verdict makes no distinction between usury and interest, between its simple and compound forms, between productive and unproductive loans, or for that matter between money and commodity borrowings. ... For the faithful it is reason enough to desist from taking or giving interest because their belief system prohibits it. But as an academic discipline Islamic economics must provide justification for the ban more so because traditionally profit and interest both go to the same functionary the capital committed to business. Why then banish one and allow the other? (Hasan; 2008; 5).*

Ashker-Wilson think there is a "definition" problem.

> *"The difficulty arises because some argue that the word Riba does not convey the meaning of interest as known nowadays, instead, it is the equivalent to usury, which connotes excessive interest (see for example, Maxime Rodinson, 1980)." (Ashley-Wilson; 2006).*

However, they rule out this argument on the ground that it does not carry conviction and conclude that: "**Riba is equivalent to interest as known to us nowadays.**" (Ashley-Wilson; 2006). Having emphasized that, they prefer to use the term "riba" instead of interest."

The Koranic riba is "loan riba which arises as a result of an increase in the amount of debt and was considered above. The "commodity riba" which arises as a result of exchange of commodities, has been stated in the Sunnah, not in the Koran. Ashker-Wilson divides the "commodity riba" into two types:

> "(a). Riba that results from exchanging an object, or a commodity, with another object of the same type, or same commodity, with an immediate delivery for an increase in quantity.

This type of Riba is called Riba al-fadle—Riba resulting from an increase in quantity of the same object in a transaction of an immediate delivery. For example, exchanging gold for gold or wheat for wheat. The exchange should not be at an increase.

(b). Riba that results from exchanging an object, of a commodity, with another object of the same type or another, same or another commodity, with a delayed delivery, future delivery. This type of Riba is called Riba al-Nasi"a—Riba resulting from an increase in quantity of the same or different object, commodity, in a transaction of a postponed, future, delivery. For example, exchanging gold for gold or wheat for wheat future delivery. The Exchange should not be at an increase. Further examples are cited below. Stating the prohibition of commodity Riba, the Prophet is reported to have clarified the exchange conditions which should be satisfied in order to avoid this Riba by saying,

> *"Gold for Gold, equivalent for equivalent;*
> *silver for silver, equivalent for equivalent;*
> *wheat for wheat, equivalent for equivalent;*
> *barely for barley, equivalent for equivalent;*
> *salt for salt, equivalent for equivalent;*
> *dates for dates equivalent for equivalent;*
>
> and whoever exceeds or asks for excess, he practiced Riba. Sell gold for silver as you wish if it is hand to hand (prompt delivery) and sell barely for dates as you wish if it is hand to hand" (flaoeioe Muslim). (Ashker-Wilson; 2006).

Based on the sayings of the Prophet, Ashker-Wilson concludes that the following general rules govern "commodity riba".

1. *"When trading metal for metal and food for food (e.g. gold for gold or wheat for wheat), two conditions must be fulfilled: (a) the quantitative equality of both objects and (b) prompt delivery.*
2. *When trading metal for metal or food for food of two different kinds (e.g. gold for silver or wheat for barely) one condition should be met: the promptness of delivery (equality is not a required condition).*
3. *When trading metal for food (gold or silver for wheat or barely) neither condition is required. The transaction is fulfilled through free trade." (Ashker-Wilson; 2006).*

One of the dissident names, Muhammed Abduh, believes that bank interest is not forbidden. There are also others. For example:

> *"A. Abdurrasul ... claims that interest on state and private company bonds is not forbidden. The underlying reason: The wisdom of prohibition of riba is to protect the weak from the powerful. Regarding bonds, interest payer is powerful (state or company), while the interest receiver (the people) is weak. Thus, a payment is made to the weak. In this connection, the usurer cannot be considered as weak.*

According to Şeltût, some Islamic lawyers consider a loan with interest acquired by the people in need as permissible. This ruling is valid for both; the state and the individuals." (Tabakoğlu; 2008; 299).

According to the "dissident" Islamic scholars like Abdülaziz Çaviş, Ismail Hakkı İzmirli, Süleyman Uludağ, Reşid Rıza and Fazlurrahman, what really prohibited is "usury, doubled and multiplied". For Ma'ruf Devalibi and Sheikh Abdülcelil, the high consumer interest rates that exploit the consumer and the poor are prohibited (see Diyanet-4). According to this view there should be no prohibition on loans to producers.

For Neccar (1978):

"All kinds of loan transactions with interest are definitely forbidden by Islam. Whether for production or consumption, all kinds of loan and credit systems are forbidden as well. […] Small or large quantity, all kinds of interest are equally forbidden."

However, Neccar quotes an exceptional case in a deep note, the limits of which are drawn by the Prophet:

'Those who have nothing to eat from morning to evening are permitted to borrow with interest.' (Buhari)" (in Neccar; 1978; 225).

On page 213 in his book, Neccar takes a standpoint promoting state financed loans with low interest rate. He says that:

"... the rationale behind this is to encourage the individuals to earn personal income and to contribute to the national income." (Neccar; 1978; 213).

He takes an even further step and says:

"The state has to provide credit to its citizens with moderate interest rate in order to develop social activities in society and to improve the exchange position." (Neccar; 1978; 213).

Karaman is one of those who think that any kind of interest which is "**unjust income or surplus**" is forbidden. Claiming that there is no difference between the interest and rent, Karaman states:

"Interest implies undeserved excess, income, rent. In secular systems where interest is free, it is considered as "deserved income"; but all divine religions prohibit it, it is forbidden. Interest if unjust and prohibited." (Karaman; 2010).

According to Ghazali quoted by S. Orman, interest is considered as a "surplus" as well.

"Literally riba implies increase and excess. As a term, it is defined as the difference between "two" financial values, an uncovered financial advantage in favor of one of the

parties in an agreement. It refers to an inequality in the trade or exchange of the same kind of objects that can be measured or calculated which implies an excess in favor of one of the parties (surplus, fazl) – or a delay in delivery when the quantities are equal (nesî'e)." (Orman; 2007; 102).

If there is an "**unjust surplus**", then there has to be an "**unjust income**", as Ghazali stated. S. Orman who quotes Ghazali states:

"Riba covers, in general, all kinds of monetary income without any service supplied." (Orman; 2007; 102).

However, what is the meaning of "service" in relation to an "unjust income"? Which practices are covered by the term "**service**" and which are excluded? As we know, the term "service" refers to non-physical, non-transportable and non-storable objects that are consumed as they are being produced, such as a hair-cut, teaching, consulting, etc. (for details see H.Gürak, 2012). Did Ghazali refer to the same kind of service? What is the criterion of "**unjust-ness**"? For instance, does the term "excess" imply a surplus in terms of "**unpaid wages**"? Or does it refer to a surplus between the nominal value and real value of a product? Or… something else?

As we can see, there are some elements of confusion on the issue of interest. "**The confusion surrounding the issue of Riba is represented particularly in commodity Riba, not the Qur'anic Riba.**" (Ashker-Wilson; 2006) which are:

1. *"Gold.*
2. *Silver.*
3. *Date.*
4. *Wheat.*
5. *Barley.*
6. *Salt.*

Some believe that the items in commodity Riba are as "numerated" in the six commodities mentioned specifically in the Sunnah. As such, the rules of commodity Riba should be confined to these while others suggest that this Riba is "exemplified" in these six commodities and it should be applied to all types of commodities, even if not mentioned in the Sunnah (Al-Qusi, op. cit.)." (Ashker-Wilson; 2006).

Interest: Reconsidered

In relation to what we learned from the Koran and the Hadiths, we can draw the following generalized conclusions:

1. Avoid receiving/paying an additional payment (interest) on loans.
2. In commodity trade, delivery must be immediate.

3. Avoid any trade involving future delivery in the commodity trade, except when the payment involves "real" money.
4. The trading of the "same" commodities must be in "equal quantities".

> *"Undoubtedly the principle reason for prohibiting interest is the the amount of excess in deals, which is in favor of one party and against the other." (Diyanet-4).*

However, up to now, there still is no consensus among the Islamic scholars on the definition, nature, scope and types of interest. The Islamic Encyclopedia shares the view on this issue:

> *"The issue of interest has been controversial from different aspects, though there is a consensus on its prohibition." (Diyanet-4).*

Nevertheless, based on the available knowledge we have two important clues that will probably be accepted by all Islamic scholars.

1. Interest is a "**surplus**", or an "**excess**" or an "**additional income**".
2. Interest is an "**unjust income**".

Now, let's look at these two important clues.

"Surplus"

It should not be any problem on having a consensus on what a "surplus" is; it refers to the gaining of an "excess quantity" from a loan or something traded, in addition to the original amount loaned or traded. Here are two examples:

Case-1: Loan interest

Assume that you lend 100 TL to someone. According to the general understanding of Islamic scholars, you should get back 100 TL if you want to avoid interest. If you get 1 TL in excess as a condition of the loan advanced, you get "interest". The payment in excess of the original loan is "**loan interest**" which is the kind of interest referred to in the Koran.

Case-2: Commodity interest

Assume that you trade wheat worth 100 kilos for a return of 101 kilos of wheat. The difference is a one kilo excess and this is called "interest" which is prohibited by the Prophet.

Let's recall the Hadith concerning the trade of dates.

"... when a sahâbî[16] *traded two scales of low quality dates for one scale of good quality dates, the Prophet ruled on that this is interest; "Avoid this! If you want to get any good quality dates, sell the low quality dates, then with that money buy the good quality dates." (Müslim, "Müsâkat", 96)" (in Diyanet-3).*

The ruling of the Prophet is the first one that refers to the selling of objects for money then to buy the desired object. Is there any essential difference? For some, the "ruled" transaction (the one referred to in the Hadith) might be the same in essence as acquiring interest. However, Islamic principles seem to consider the selling and buying process using money as correct. Remember what the Koran has to say on trade and interest: "**trade is permissible, interest is prohibited**". If a barter exchange is intended, then the objects of trade must be "the same", the quantities "equal" and the delivery "immediate".

In the case where different objects are the subject of trade, e.g. wheat for gold, barley for silver, there is no requirement for "equal quantities" or "immediate" delivery.

Now it is time to consider the term "**surplus**" in connection with the term "**unjust income**". The term "**unearned income**" will be considered to be synonymous with "**unjust income**".

1- "Earned" Income

What we mean by "earned income" is the income gained in return for a product produced or sold and the labor expended to do a job. "Earned income" of an entrepreneur has to contain the labor expended and the risk assumed.

In the Islamic literature, generally, reference is made to "**just (halal) income**" rather than "**unjust (haram) income**" which is equivalent to the term "unearned income". The Islamic term "halal income" refers to income obtained through means consistent with Islamic principles. Although earned and unearned do not mean exactly the same thing as the Islamic halal and haram incomes, we shall prefer the terms "**earned- unearned incomes**" since they give us the opportunity to cover the analysis of the income of non-Muslims, as well.

The use of labor-power in the supply of products is a "causa sine qua non". Nothing would be supplied in the markets in the absence of the use of labor-power, ranging from the supply of physical goods such as cars, telephones, etc., to services such as teaching, cleaning, etc. Islamic sources also acknowledge the

---

16 Sahâbî: a Muslim who has seen or if blind, talked with the Prophet when he was alive.

indispensable role of laborer in production: "**The principle factor of production according to Islam is the "labor"** (Diyanet-3). Therefore, the wage gained is definitely an "**earned income**".

However, nowadays laborer alone is not sufficient to supply products or to carry out a job. For example, in order to supply various products, the laborer utilizes and/or transforms the gifts of nature (raw materials). Some of the transformed inputs of production are tools, machinery, etc., which in turn are the intermediary inputs and "capital goods", e.g., "other" inputs for production.

In order to initiate the supply of products, there is a need for "capital" which brings together the laborer and all the "other" inputs of production. The driving force motivating the "capital owner" to supply various goods and services is the "surplus" or "profit" motive. Since the outcome of production in terms of profit is uncertain, the capital owner assumes some "risk". The surplus in return for the "risk" assumed can also be considered as "**earned income**".

Thus, there are to qualifications regarding the "**earned income**":

1. Spending labor power.
2. Assuming "**risk**" related to undertaking a production.

2- "Unearned income"

"**Unearned income**" is the type of income that does not contain any of the labor effort or the risks involved. For example, an increase in the amount of savings passively kept in a bank is "interest income" and can be considered as "**unearned income**". That is because; the money produces money.

Let's consider some types of "unearned incomes".

Case-1

Assume that a man named Zafer borrows 1,000 TL for a week from a friend named Mustafa. Next week Zafer pays back 1,000 TL, the exact amount he borrowed. During the past week Zafer bought an object worth 1,000 TL and sold it for 1,200 TL making 200 TL profit. Is Zafer's "surplus" income after one week an earned income or an unearned income?

One might argue that: "Mustafa could enter a partnership with Zafer and acquire half of the profit, 100 TL." If Zafer asked Mustafa to enter a partnership but Mustafa refused, then the additional income can be considered as "earned income". But, what if Zafer never mentioned the business opportunity to Mustafa so he could keep the entire "surplus" for himself? Can we still say that Zafer's income is "earned"?

Mustafa who credited the money to Zafer may say he is content because he values the good deed more than any surplus. But the question here is whether Zafer's additional income of 200 TL is permissible or not.

Case-2

Bayındır who quotes Ebu Yusuf claims that if 10 kilos of expensive wheat is borrowed and then paid back when wheat is cheaper, the transaction will lead to "**unjust-ness**". Here is the rationale of Ebu Yusuf, according to Bayındır:

> *"If the value of borrowed fungible goods increase or decrease due to a price rise or for other reasons, they should be repaid at the value valid on the day of lending." (Bayındır; 2009).*

Within the context of negative interest, Islamic Encyclopedia presents a similar standpoint on the issue: **an interest rate below the inflation rate should be considered within the scope of prohibited interest**. (Diyanet-4).

The related questions are: how to compensate an unjust surplus in favor of the one or the other, as a result of price fluctuations? How can one determine the magnitude of "unjust-ness"? If the quality of the borrowed goods changed due to the introduction of a new technology, how can one evaluate or measure the extent of "surplus" income? Is the surplus an "**earned or unearned**" income?

Case-3

According to an Hadith on the commodity interest, gold for gold must be traded in equal quantities and with immediate delivery.

> *"During the period of the Prophet, the gold currency was named dinar of which the weight was about four grams gold. If anyone desired to buy jewelry with that gold currency, it would, in fact, be a trade of gold for gold. In this conjunction, if we buy a bracelet weighing 40 grams gold by paying 15 dinars which is equivalent to 60 grams gold, the difference of 20 grams would be "surplus". (http-13).*

According to the example above, the bracelet must weigh 60 grams to avoid any interest. Only then there will be "equality" and no "surplus" or "unearned income" will occur. But, would it be a "halal" (permissible) transaction to buy a bracelet weighing 60 grams gold for 15 dinars also weighing 60 grams of gold, if the bracelet contains the labor of a goldsmith on it? Would the ignoring value added to the bracelet by the labor not be "not permissible"?

Regarding the gold trade, the Ilmihal of Diyanet states:

"... the workmanship on the processed gold is disregarded. Therefore, a processed gold cannot be traded for gold superior in weight on account of the workmanship expended on it." (Diyanet-3).

Is this conclusion of the Islamic Encyclopedia a "just" one capable of preventing injustice?

Assume that a goldsmith spends five hours of his labor time worth 10 dinars to process a bracelet. What should be the market price of the bracelet weighing 60 grams gold?

60 grams gold = 15 Dinars
5 hours' labor = 10 Dinars

The price of a 60 gram gold bracelet would be:

= 15 Dinar + 10 Dinar = **25 Dinar**

Who would trade this processed bracelet for 15 dinars? Can a trade that ignores the contribution of human labor be "permissible"? These kinds of transactions seem to be in need of clarification by the Islamic scholars who have the final say on religious issues.

Anyone who is familiar with the supply of products, whether she/he is an economist, a businessman or a layman, would know that the most important, valuable and significant input of any production is the labor effort expended on a product. (For a detailed argument, see Gürak; 2012). This is confirmed by the Ilmihal of the Diyanet:

"In Islam, the principal source of production is the "labor". (Diyanet-3).

Who can claim that Islam does not value the man's labor?

Let's recall what the Prophet said once when asked which the "most valuable income" is; he said:

"Those earned by labor effort and commerce." (http-12).

Case-4

Once upon a time, the currencies in use were the dinar, gold money, and the dirham, silver money. Both reflected the value of the metal contained. For instance dinar contained four grams of gold. Today, we do not use this kind of currency anymore. Today's global monetary system is based on "paper money". The most widely used currency around the world is the "paper" US Dollar. Every year, the Fed of the USA prints billions of Dollars to be used around the world in various transactions. And, as we know, the printing cost of a $ 100 or $ 200 bill is just a few cents, a lot lower than its nominal value.

We live in an age where, in practice, all Central Banks intervene in the markets one way or another, influencing economic indicators. How can one evaluate properly the "unjustness" and "unearned incomes" in a financial world like this? And, how do we do it?

Case-5

According to an Islamic web site:

> *"... those goods which are not measurable or can be weighed, but countable or measurable in meters, are not subject to interest. Accordingly, for the mobile phones interest is not applicable. Therefore, it is not interest if one mobile phone is traded for two. (http-14).*

In this approach to trade, the labor effort of the worker is ignored. What is the criterion for trading one mobile phone for two? Obviously, it is not the weights of the mobile phones which determine their relative values? If there is no "just" criterion to determine the market price of phones, the trade will always be open to "unjust incomes" or "unfair transactions".

Chapter-7

Interest, Surplus, Savings and Rent

Introduction

This section concerns:

1. The definition of the interest, i.e., the definition of the "additional" payment (a surplus) to the original amount of debt loaned to the end-user, the rate of which is predetermined.
2. Whether the "additional", i.e. the "surplus income" obtained by the creditor is "**earned**" **or** "**unearned**" **income**.
3. Interest-Rent relationship.

The "additional" amount or "surplus" can be paid to the creditor in instalments or at one go. All that matters here is the "surplus" payment in addition to the loan advanced. For example, if one borrows 100 TL and pays back 101 TL, a "surplus" will be paid to the creditor. The loan institutions concerned are the Western type financial institutions; so the activities of the Islamic financial institutions are not being dealt with at this time. However some of the conclusions may be beneficial to Islamic economics and Islamic financial institutions.

Income of the Financial Firms

Let's recap what we discussed in the previous section.

The income of a manufacturer of cars, computers, or shirts i.e., the manufacturer of a commodity or a service has been defined as "**earned income**" which is equivalent to the profit after taxes have been paid. That is because the producer assumes a risk and employs laborer(s) which justifies the profit obtained. The indispensable input of any production is the laborer. The laborer receives a wage in return for his labor "effort". Taking the entire production process into consideration, three conditions have to be met in order for the income to be categorized as "**earned income**".

1. Labor effort.
2. Production.
3. Risk.

When economists make a reference to "production", the first thing that springs to mind is, usually, the supply of physical products. But, output activities in commerce, (which was the profession exercised by the Prophet Muhammad) and many other economic activities such as tourism, education, etc., are "service" activities. Whenever we refer to "production" in this section, we mean the supply of both physical goods and services. [17].

The main difference between a commodity supply and a service supply is that the latter is consumed as it is produced. A service supplied cannot be stored or transported. For example, a trader in Turkey may export cars or shirts to Sweden and earn a profit. There is no "physical" addition to the value of a car or a shirt by the trader which would change the original substance of the object; that is because the trader only "produces" a service. However, while producing a service, the trader, normally, employs laborer and some capital. Whether the producer utilizes his/her own labor effort or capital does not essentially affect the outcome. That is because; in both cases, labor effort is employed and production related risk is assumed. Therefore, the income obtained as a result of "labor effort, production and risk" is considered as "**earned income**".

Financial institutions perform the function of an intermediary in the financing of production of the supply of commodities and services. In addition, they also contribute to increase output indirectly by providing credit for the consumer. While supplying a "**financial service**", financial institutions employ "laborer" and take on the related risk involved. That is to say, a financial institution not only uses "labor effort" but also takes on the "risk of a loss". Under these circumstances, it would not be unjustified to consider the additional income of a financial institution as "profit" or "**earned additional income**".

Essentially, there is no real distinction between the service supplied in commerce and the service supplied by the finance sector in terms of "labor input, production or risk". The additional income in the financial sector is known as "interest", in general, but it is known as "profit" within the sector.

In short; considered from the point of view of the labor expended and the risk assumed there is no difference in reality between a service supplied in the financial sector and other service's activities. A trading company supplies a "service"; so does the financial sector. Thus, it is justified to call the income in service sector "**earned income**".

The "Surplus" in the Return of a Loan

Based on the previous argument, the income which the financial intermediaries accrue from their service (subject to labor input and risk assumption) is

17 For a detailed analysis of distinction between the supply of physical goods and services, see H. Gürak, 2012, "Economics".

now considered as “**earned income**”. However, is it rational to describe all types of income which the financial intermediaries accrue in the return of a loan as “earned”? The discussions below are aimed to shed light on this question.

1- Loans for “Production” and the “Surplus”

All investments which aim to supply a commodity or a service are important for the wealth and the developmental level of a society. While some investments can be realized with a relatively small amount of capital[18], others require large capital investments, especially in the sectors of advanced technology and those requiring large scale output. The investor may not always be able to raise the full amount of capital required for the “new” or “additional” investment from his or her internal resources. In such a case, the investor may have to seek an “external” source. In some cases, i.e., competitive survival or in the development of a “new” technology, it may be absolutely necessary to use “external” resources in order to survive the competitive threat.

In some cases this “external” capital is supplied by “savers” who assume the ordinary risk of a profit or loss by purchasing shares in the firm. Thereby the suppliers of the “new” capital become co-owners of the production unit and deserve a part of the profits or a share in the loss. But it is not always easy to acquire “new” capital in such a way or the entrepreneur, for some reason, may not prefer this kind of solution. In this case, a financial intermediary may enter the scene and supply the “external” capital by lending his money in return of a pre-determined rate of “surplus” or “additional” payment for the credit he advanced. The financial intermediary supplying the “external” capital as credit is, usually, a bank which utilizes the “passive” savings accumulated in its bank deposits. But, occasionally, even the Central Bank may appear as the supplier of the needed capital.

What justifies this “pre-determined” rate of “surplus”? The financial intermediary which places some of the deposit savings at the disposal of an investor supplies a service and assumes the risk of a loss. This “risk assumption”, in a way, and to some extent, implies sharing the borrowing investor’s risk in his production enterprise. If the investor suffers a loss, so does the financial intermediary. In the case of a default in the payment of the loan the financial intermediary suffers accordingly. Therefore, for the credit service supplied (which involves the risk of loss and the cost of the “labor effort” of the employees), the financial intermediary demands a “predetermined” rate of “surplus” on the loan advanced. This is

18 For a detailed description of the term capital, see H. Gürak, “Economics”, 2012.

commonly known as "interest". In other words, the financial intermediary which **produces a service** expends the **labor effort of his employees** and assumes **risk of loss**. As Ghazali states; "**... no gains are justified without the risk of loss.**" (Ghazali; 1994; 50).

The financial intermediary makes an "indirect" contribution to the supply of the commodity or the service produced by the investor receiving the loan. Under these circumstances, it would not be unfair or unjust to categorize the "surplus" income of a financial intermediary as "**earned income**". That is because; all the three conditions of "**earned income**" are fulfilled. What a trading company does is, essentially the same; it employs laborer to supply a service which bears the risk of a loss.

2- Loans for "Consumption" and the "Surplus"

One of the major activities of a financial intermediary is lending money to the consumer. By doing this, a financial intermediary contributes to sustaining the supply and demand of some products to a certain extent. The purpose of the borrower may be to meet a basic demand or the satisfaction of a desire. If the purpose is to satisfy a desire, this can be postponed to a later date. For instance, when someone borrows money to buy a car, a smart-TV or a mobile phone, it is not usually to meet a basic or urgent need. So, if this "consumption desire" were to be postponed, there would be no need borrow and to pay a pre-determined "surplus" (interest) in addition to the original amount of loan.

However, nowadays, the demand for non-basic products appears to have reached incredible levels. As a matter of fact, for many individuals, regardless of their level of income, possessing a car, a TV-set or a mobile phone with a well-known brand-name seems to be a "**psychological necessity**"; or perhaps individuals are driven to think that way. To them, possessing products with a well-known brand-name appears to be a way of acquiring a "higher status" in society. The more they possess or consume such products, the more distinguished and successful they think they will be. When their income is insufficient, borrowing money and paying interest presents no problem for them. It appears that, NOT being able to borrow is a greater hardship for them.

Nobody can force anybody to borrow or to consume more. Individuals make the choice of borrowing and paying a "surplus" in addition to the loan by their own free will. It would be unfair to blame a financial intermediary for lending money and getting a "surplus". Besides, there is always the risk of a default in payment. Since the financial intermediary supplies a service through his employees and assumes a risk, and the consumer uses his own free will to make a decision, it may not be fair to label the "surplus" income as "**unearned income**". Obviously, this matter needs further and detailed consideration.

3- Loans for "Basic Consumption" and the "Surplus"

Needing to borrow to meet the "basic" needs is not only an economic matter but also a moral matter which concerns the whole of humanity. In our age today, in a civilized country, all the "basic" requirements such as food, shelter, health and clothing of all individuals in need, should be met and guaranteed by the state. Nobody should ever need to borrow to meet such necessities. If an individual has no choice but to borrow and pay a "surplus" to meet his/her basic needs then the society in which that individual lives does not deserve to be called a "civilized" society.

"Technically", if somebody takes advantage of the needy and lends money which requires the payment of interest, the additional income may be defined as "earned income" since money lender provides a service that involves labor effort and risk. The state of the borrower or the person(s) in basic needs is a reprehensible and undesirable state of affairs. If a person is in this state, it is the society as a whole who is responsible in the first place for not eliminating this problem. Assuming that the society has not fulfilled its duty, and a financial institution takes advantage of this, then on "moral-ethical" grounds, such income may be defined as "unearned income" as the loan is to meet the "basic requirements.

4- Loans Borrowed by the State and the "Surplus"

From time to time, any state may borrow money in order to cover a state budget deficit or to spend on certain things. In the case of developing countries, most of the time they pay a "surplus" or an interest rate above the going market rate. The reason for borrowing may be an unexpected economic cycle, the structure of global economic relationships, corruption or inefficient governance. In order to overcome the problem the state may have to print money, borrow money, increase taxes or cut the expenditure.

According to the understanding of most economists, printing money is not a desirable solution and presents more problems in the future. Generally what is advised, is borrowing from internal and external sources in order to keep the economy stable and to avoid cyclical ups and downs. However, though borrowing may seem like a rational decision in the beginning, the "surplus" (interest) payments on loans can become an extremely heavy burden in the future. The major reason for this burden is the payment of an excessive "surplus" (interest). This is especially the case in the developing countries. The money lenders (usually Western countries or their institutions) are not unaware of this problem that is the effect caused by these heavy, above average market rate, "surplus" payments on developing countries. It is well-known that the debt ratio in some countries is higher than their GDP. Some people claim that Western countries deliberately choose such a debt and interest policy to make the borrowing country politically and economically ever more dependent on the lender.

Increasing the taxes or cutting public expenditure is among the options. However, in general, the public does not seem to favor either of these options.

Can borrowing be avoided? Certainly! When things are going well in an economy, the related state organs can put aside some money for future "precautionary" expenditure. However, this kind of measures does not seem to be popular in modern societies. Selfish individuals prefer "today's benefit" to "tomorrow's benefit".

Perhaps, when a state's economy faces such a situation, it would be rational to explain the situation to the public in detail, present possible solutions and seek their approval regarding the chosen policy. They could for example take a vote with regard to several possible resolutions, including the interest payment on a loan or a tax increase to overcome the budget deficit problem or to reduce public expenditure.

Whenever the decision is made to borrow, the outcome is obvious; a pre-determined rate "surplus" has to be paid in addition to the loan. The money lender meets a demand while the borrower makes a conscious choice" thinking that this is his most rational solution. The lender supplies a service, expends labor and assumes the risk. But there is no direct contribution to the supply of goods or services. Under the circumstances, it is not easy to categorize the surplus income (interest) of the lender whether it is an "**earned or unearned income**". After all, there is a labor effort and a risk assumption involved.

The "Surplus" on Saving Deposits of Individuals[19]

For financial enterprises it is customary to pay a pre-determined rate of additional payment to the owners of deposit accounts, especially to the time-deposit or interest accounts. This additional payment to the depositor displays a feature

19 We assume that there is no inflation, unless otherwise stated.

distinct from the additional payment made to financial enterprises. Though both are known or referred to as "interest", the difference is that the depositor neither spends any labor effort nor produces any added value through production. As a matter of fact, the deposited money produces more money (money hoarding).

There are four options for a money hoarder?

Option-1: The depositor may start a new business or join an existing business in order to supply goods or services and directly assume the risk of profit or loss. If profit is obtained as a result of a direct contribution to production by employing laborer, then the additional income in terms of profit can be defined as "**earned income**".

Option-2: The savings may be kept in a deposit account in a financial enterprise and receive a pre-determined rate of "surplus" known as interest. This option has nothing to do with producing anything or employing any labor. This kind of "surplus" accrues solely from owning the money. Therefore, this type of income is defined as "**unearned income**".

Some economists claim that the savings deposited in a financial enterprise make an indirect contribution to the supply of goods and services. That is correct. However, the output related risks are not assumed by the depositor. What matters for the depositor is the pre-determined rate of "surplus", e.g., interest. In a case of default in payments from the loan receiver, it is not the depositor but the financial intermediary who normally would be affected. As a matter of fact the risk, if any, facing the depositor may be minimized by insuring the deposited amount. For example, in Turkey, all deposits up to 50,000 TL are under the protection of a state guarantee. Ignoring the risk of bankruptcy of the financial enterprise, the interest receiving money holder does not fulfill any of the conditions to obtain an "**earned income**" i.e., there is no involvement in production and no labor effort.

Option-3: The savings may be kept in a private vault or "under the pillow" making no contribution to output or employment. There is no "surplus" income either, because the savings are "non-productive". Keeping savings in such a way is of no use to its owner or to society. Islam does not approve of non-productive savings.

Option-4: Savings can be spent to consume available goods and services thus making an indirect contribution to production.

To summarize; the savings that do not contribute to the supply of goods or services are "**unproductive savings**". Any additional income to such savings involves neither labor effort nor any production related risk. Therefore, they should be categorized as "**unearned income**".

Encouraging Productive Investment

A credit policy that encourages the "**productive**" employment of financial resources while, at the same time, discouraging the "**unproductive**" would be a highly beneficial system to long term economic growth and to increase prosperity. A rational credit policy should always aim to increase the use of savings in the production of goods and services. By doing this, society will benefit more from savings in terms of increased employment, competition and welfare.

An Hypothesis

Assume an economic system in which any "surplus" payment made to any kind of saving deposits is prohibited by law. What would be the likely outcome of such a decision? Would investments be affected positively or negatively?

Whenever a "surplus" (interest) payment is made to the deposited savings, the cost of borrowing for investment from a financial intermediary is bound to increase. This credit cost would, naturally, increase the unit cost of production of any goods or services supplied, for which credit is used. Assume that the average market interest rate paid for savings deposited is 10 percent. Then the cost of borrowing must be at least 10 percent to cover the expense of the financial enterprise.

Further assume that the transaction cost of a financial enterprise which lends the money to the investor is 3 percent. Under the circumstance, the minimum cost of borrowing will amount to 13 percent. Like any commercial enterprise, the financial institution would expect to earn some profit from the transaction, say 15 percent. Then the minimum total cost of a loan for a break-even point, excluding taxes, has to be 28 percent (10+3+15=28), maybe even higher cet. par.

If the interest rate on saving deposits were zero, given the transaction cost of 3 percent and 15 percent profit of the financial enterprise, the total cost, e.g., the interest rate, on the loan would be 18 percent, 10 percent lower than the case where interest is paid on the savings. This result would imply a lower cost of production in the supply of goods and services produced by the loans. And the major beneficiaries would be the consumers who would have to pay less for the same products, cet. par.

Another negative effect of interest payment on savings would be on the potential demand for goods and services. When savings are deposited to receive interest, the potential consumption would, quite likely, be lower than in the case without interest. That is because; the owners of savings would postpone their consumption to a future date.

Another positive impact of a lower credit cost would be on the sale price of the product supplied by credit, which in turn would affect competition and employment. That is because; lower cost of production implies lower sale price, higher competition and more employment, cet. par.

Assume a financial system where deposit savings are not rewarded by a "surplus" (interest). The probability of having a negative impact on the on the economy as a whole is expected to be low, if not unlikely. On the contrary, the expected positive benefits would be invaluable. In an interest free system on deposit savings, the owners of the savings:

1. Either; would have to join the producers in supplying goods and services to obtain a profit.
2. Or they would keep their savings idle and obtain no additional income.
3. Or spend the savings.

When the first option is preferred by the savers, some goods or services will have to be produced, laborers employed and risk assumed. Then the income will be "**earned**".

When the second option is preferred there will be no contribution to output, no labor expended and no output related risk assumed. Since the possibility of earning money by holding money is eliminated in an interest free financial system, there would not be any benefit to society or to the money holder, except for cases of emergency. If there is inflation, the purchasing-power of the savings will diminish gradually.

When the third option is preferred, there will be an indirect contribution to the increased supply of goods and services through increased demand, assuming that the market has not yet saturated.

In short, in a financial system where "unproductive" savings are not rewarded by a pre-determined rate of interest, a great part of the savings would be diverted into either increased production or increased consumption. In this case, both, the producers as well as consumer would be the main beneficiaries of such an interest-free system.

"Hoarding" Money, Capital & Competition

As is well known most Islamic economists consider the getting or paying of interest as prohibited. Now assume that an Islamic producer in a competitive market wants to develop a new technology in a dynamic sector that requires large sums of money. Further assume that the Islamic producers' own financial resources are not sufficient to realize the investment to develop the new technology and looks for an external resource to raise the money. This would naturally require the payment of interest on the loan. But since paying "interest" is against his faith, he/she cannot get credit with interest on it. He/she may attempt to get the required amount from Muslims who have accumulated financial funds and kept them "under the pillow". But, this isn't as easy as it sounds. That is because hoarding money and keeping it idle under the pillow is not a permissible behavior. The Sunnah "Repentance" says:

> *"And there are those who hoard gold and silver and spend it not in the Way of Allah: announce unto them a most grievous chastisement...*
>
> *On the Day when it will be heated in the fire of Hell, and with it will be branded their foreheads, their flanks, and their backs.- "This is the (treasure) which ye hoarded for yourselves: taste ye, then, the (treasures) ye buried!" (Repentance-9; 34 & 35).*

The non-Muslim competitors can easily borrow the required amount from the bank for the same purpose and strengthen his/her competitive position. In the end, the non-Muslim competitor would be in a position to eliminate the Muslim competitor, driving him/her out of the market. Thus the faithful behavior of the Muslim competitor may be very costly to him/her and to the Muslim economy at large.

According to Western mainstream economic doctrine and the nature of the relationships in the existing economic system, individuals have to be "selfish" in maximizing their personal gain, a typical Homo Economicus behavior. Yet, according to the basic principles of Islam, individuals have to be just the opposite of Homo Economicus; i.e. "unselfish" or altruistic. Doing things for others is a highly praised and virtuous behavior. For example, a producer in the mainstream economic doctrine does not care what really happens to the competitors. In fact, an efficient producer aims to "destroy", or if you will, eliminate all competitors from the market in order to maximize personal gain. Yet, according to the Islamic understanding, even the competitors should act with solidarity. Examples of such solidarity could be seen in the Turkish "**Ahi**" system where a producer was expected to say: "**Today, I earned enough for my family; let the "others" earn a livelihood, too**" in the event that the "others" hadn't earned enough. This kind of thinking is ethically praiseworthy, but it would not be an "appropriate" way of thinking when entering into competitive transactions with Western minded business people. Western minded business people would wipe them off the market in no time and at every opportunity.

Rent

Rent is a kind of income subject to unending moral as well as economic arguments. Three kinds of rent will be analyzed below.

1. One kind of rent is related to "excessive" profits above the market average arising from such **imperfect market conditions** as black-markets, cartels, oligopoly, and monopoly. Under such imperfect market conditions, the end-users usually have to pay a higher than normal price which increases the profits above the "normal" profit-level without any additional costs or efforts. Since this type "additional" income does not involve any labor effort or competitive risks, it can be categorized as "**unearned**" income when compared to our definition of "earned" income.
2. Another type of income categorized as rent is related to the **ownership of property**, such as land, building, flats, etc. For instance, the owner of a piece of land may obtain income, as a result of the efforts of those who actually toil the land. Income accruing may be in the form of money or "in kind", like crop-sharing.
   Or, in a similar fashion, the owner of a building or a flat may let out the owned property for a pre-determined amount of money for a given period and receive an income called "rent". Such types of incomes can be categorized as "**earned**" income, provided that the property is, in the first place, acquired through legal and just means, and the cost of property fully paid.
3. A third kind of rent arises as a result of "Ricardian" style differences in the productivity of the land due to the differing natural qualities of the land. Assume that there two equal sized pieces of land with different qualities. The same quality and amount of inputs are used to grow tomatoes in both areas. But the first area is assumed to be 20 percent more fertile (productive) per unit, which implies a higher level of income and profit rate for the owner. Since this kind of rent income is caused by market conditions, the income can be categorized as "**fair income**" meaning that the income is in compliance with the legislation. But it does not qualify to be described as "**earned income**", because there is no extra labor effort involved or risk assumed.
   The differences in income from rented buildings or flats of equal size but in different locations can be treated similarly. For instances, the rental price of a flat in a suburb is normally lower than a flat of equal size in the town-center. There seems to be no economic or logical ground to classify such rental income differences as "**unfair income**" because the income is in compliance with the legislation. However, the extra income can be classified

as "**unearned**" because there is no labor inputs nor any risk assumption in getting the extra income.

Rent as an "extra income" as in the Case-1 and Case-2 stated above is an income **not obtained by additional efforts of labor or "competitive risk assumption but simply by a monopoly position and/or ownership**. Therefore the extra income does not qualify to be called "**earned income**". Can interest be called "rent" similar to the Cases 1 and 2 above?

Rent-Interest Dichotomy?

Let's recall that three conditions have to be met in order for the income to be categorized as "**earned income**".

1. Labor effort.
2. Production.
3. Risk.

In the previous paragraphs in this Chapter on interest, reference was made to several types of "additional" incomes some of which were classified as "earned" and some as "unearned" income in conjunction with the three conditions stated above. In this context, some types of extra incomes such as the "additional income" on the passive saving deposits receiving income in the form of "interest" may be considered as "rent" equivalent to the Cases 1 and 2 above. However, following the same argument, the income of a bank employing laborer and assuming competitive risk would not qualify as "rent" in that sense, but as "unearned income". Therefore, as stated before, what a commercial bank earns is "profit" not interest or rent.

"Interest" vs. "Profit-sharing"

So far, we have not made any comments on the Islamic Financial System or Islamic Banking. However, it is high time to express some remarks on an issue relevant to our topic, which we discus sed in this section; that is the subject of "profit-sharing". We believe that there is an interesting resemblance between the "**prohibited interest**" and the "**non-prohibited profit-share**" paid to the money-holder in the Islamic Banking System under the heading "profit-loss share".

As we already know, in Islam it is prohibited to pay the money-lender an "**additional pre-determined rate of income**", i.e., interest. The underlying reasons for the prohibition are that the money-lender neither expends any labor-effort, nor assumes any "direct" risk related to the supply of any product. The hoarded (accumulated)-money increases with an additional amount of income which is not "earned", cet. par.

On these grounds the Islamic Financial System avoids the payment of any kind of interest. However, the system does not object to a similar payment under the heading of "**profit-loss share**". The payment is a "**pre-determined rate of additional income**" known as "profit-share". There are several so called "Islamic" financial enterprises established in Turkey, the annual "**pre-determined rate profit-sharing**" of which in May-2014 was about 6-7 percent for time-deposits for a month.

Those who see no problem with the payment of a "**pre-determined rate of additional income (profit-share)**" claim that this is a payment arising in conjunction with the "profit-loss share" system. The question is; who knows, in advance, that the annual rate of return for the enterprise is going to be a profit or a loss? What is the essential difference between the pre-determined interest rate and the pre-determined profit-share? What if the enterprise makes an annual rate of profit of 20 percent? Or 2 percent? The answers to the following questions are vital from an Islamic point of view.

1. Would there not be a case to be made that this is just the same as an interest payment.
2. Would it not contain a risk for one of the parties of getting some unearned-income, which is considered as abhorrent in the Islamic system?
3. Do those who receive a "profit-share" expend any labor-effort?
4. Do those who receive a "profit-share" assume any "direct" risk in the supply of any product?

Final Remarks on Interest

An attempt has been made in this section to reconsider and reevaluate the concept "surplus income" or, alternatively "additional payment". Income is divided into two categories:

1. **Unearned income** obtained without making any labor effort, supplying any product or assuming any supply related risk.
2. **Earned income** obtained by expending labor, engaging in production and assuming a supply related risk.

Two distinctive features of "**unearned income**" should not be overlooked; "**not expending any labor effort**" and "**not supplying any product**", in other words, not assuming any production related risk. On the other hand, an "**earned income**" had two distinctive features; "**labor input**" and "**production**" along with production related risks.

Among these two types of incomes, the promotion of "earned income" seems to be economically more rational, and ethically more just and fair. That is because; the system prevents the opportunity of making more money from an available money stock. Such an interest-free financial system as discussed above seems to be in compliance with the Islamic tenets.

Chapter-8

Concluding Remarks

We observed, in different sections of this book, that there are no comprehensive and universally applicable Islamic "scientific" economic theories, which appeal not only to Muslim communities but also to non-Muslim communities. Although the analysis is not included in our study, we can assert, based on the general perception, that the neither the political system nor the human rights records of many, if not the majority of so called "Islamic" countries, reveal "good" records for both the Muslims and non-Muslims. In other words, there seems to be no appropriate role-model community including both Muslims and non-Muslims; at least not for the present.

One of the main reasons to account for the present undesired circumstances might be the failure of Islamic scholars to develop "new" ideas to deal with the contemporary issues properly. The "new" and up to date ideas should not only be in the field of economics but in all fields of life, ranging from politics to cosmology, from producer rights/obligations to administrative issues, etc.

Whenever Islamic rulers or scholars encounter some tough issues, they seem to seek guidance in the Golden Age of Islam during the rule of the Prophet and four Caliphs which lasted for a very short period of time (about 1,400 years ago). "Returning to the holy period" and to the circumstances applicable at that time is, in practice, just nostalgic wishful thinking rather than a practical solution. After all, about 1,400 years has passed and both inter- and intra- societal relationships have changed radically over the course of time. Certainly there are many useful lessons to be learned from the past. But, now we live in a "new and totally different age". In this "new" age, we need "new" ideas and "new" remedies.

Naturally Islamic scholars might assume that one day the entire world population will convert to Islam. Only then, will there be two main common sources of living and inspiration; the Koran and the Sunnah. From then on, any choice of action will be based not only on the immediate reward in this life but also on those rewards in the hereafter. Accordingly the way of living and comprehending this life will be totally different. But we don't know yet when that day will come. Until then, Islamic economists must strive to develop comprehensive "alternative" economic theories which would change the conventional understanding of non-Islamic economies and their way of life.

General Perception

There are about 60 countries where the majority of the population is Muslim. Some of them claim to be ruled according to Islamic laws and principles. In fact, some refer to themselves as "Islamic" states. For example; the Iranian Islamic

Republic, the Islamic Republic of Afghanistan, the Islamic Republic of Pakistan, the Islamic Republic of Mauritania. On the other hand, there are countries such as the State of Qatar and the Kingdom of Saudi Arabia that do not bear the title "Islamic" but the rulers claim to implement Islamic law and principles. And, there are also "secular" countries like the Republic of Turkey and the Republic of Azerbaijan that are ruled by a secular constitution.

Judging from the evidence at hand, there is no Islamic society ruled by Islamic law in which Muslims can proudly say; "this is the ideal society" which conforms to every aspect of the tenets of Islam. Some countries may claim to be ruled by true Islamic tenets but the degree of their achievements is dubious in many respects. What has been done and achieved so far does not seem qualify them as an "ideal" society.

Let us give an example to one of the shortcomings in practice. According to the Islamic religion, all Muslims are brothers and sisters and they should act in solidarity with each other. Spending the halal income in the way of Allah is an excellent example of acting with solidarity. Allah declares in the Koran:

> *"It is not righteousness that ye turn your faces towards East or West; but it is righteousness- to believe in Allah and the Last Day, and the Angels, and the Book, and the Messengers; to spend of your substance, out of love for Him, for your kin, for orphans, for the needy, for the wayfarer, for those who ask, and for the ransom of slaves; to be steadfast in prayer, and give Zakat (regular charity); to fulfill the contracts which ye have made; and to be firm and patient, in pain (or suffering) and adversity, and throughout all periods of panic. Such are the people of truth, the God fearing." (Baqara-2:177).*

> *"They ask thee what they should spend (In charity). Say: Whatever wealth ye spend that is good, is for parents and kindred and orphans and those in want and for wayfarers. And whatever ye do that is good, -Allah knoweth it well." (Baqara-2:215).*

Can anyone claim that Muslims act with solidarity in real life, as Allah has commanded? Let us be more specific. There are some extremely rich countries that claim to be Islamic. Some of the rulers of these countries are considered among the richest in the world. Their accessories in the bath rooms of their houses are of pure gold, as we see in the media. They own not one or two luxury cars but many. They travel in expensive private airplanes, spending money without limit. On the other hand, there are many poor countries where Muslims are in urgent need of the basic requirements to have a decent life. Under these circumstances, can anyone claim that Muslims live and act in solidarity?

Acting in solidarity is a humane and ethical issue. Muslim or non-Muslim, all "civilized" societies should act in solidarity with each other. But, since solidarity is one of the crucial issues for an Islamic society, can the Islamic economists proudly say that they have done all they can to facilitate the emergence and development of an “**ideal society for the whole of mankind**”, i.e. for Muslim or non-Muslim alike, with appropriate policy measures and appropriate instruments of government? On the development of Islamic economics, S. Orman remarks:

> *“We have to admit that the theoretical attempts in Islamic economics so far has been in a kind of* **Islamisizing of knowledge**, *rather than developing knowledge. To put it differently, the attempts in this field have been in the form of pillaging the available knowledge, adapting it for the building an Islamic economic system or, as sometimes stated, the mere Islamization of knowledge, rather than making attempts to* create new knowledge.” *(Orman; 2013-a).*

There are some attempts by some Islamic economists like M.F. Khan, M.A. Zar ga, M. Iqbal, S. Tahir, A.H.Sulaiman to create an “**Islamic School of Economics**”. However, they seem to be at the infant stage and thus inadequate to be considered as a serious challenge to Western economics. If Islamic economists and those Islamic scholars interested in economic matters, aim to develop “**new Islamic economic ideas**”, addressing and embracing the whole of mankind, regardless of religious commitment, they should start by developing a globally acknowledged “value-price theory” in compliance with Islamic tenets. That is because; the value-price theory is the basis of all other economic theories. In the absence of an alternative but realistic, rational and comprehensive value-price theory, other related economic theories are bound to be unproductive, unable to explain actual events or unable to offer any sound policy measures; just like Western mainstream economics. The aim of Islamic economists should not be in creating yet “**another**” **system of “blackboard economics**”.

Final Remarks: Competence

One of the important religious principles in Islam is that a job that has to be done should be given to the “**most competent**” person(s) endowed with the appropriate skills, education and experience to do it most efficiently. The discipline of economics and all related matters are no exception to that principle. Who are the most competent persons in economic matters? The answer is obvious; those who possess the right background in terms of education, skill and experience. Therefore, society should always pay attention and take into consideration all ideas, comments and explanations of the competent experts in economics. For example, regarding the matter of “interest”, the Diyanet (the council that oversees religious pronouncements in Turkey) says:

> *“... in order to specify some criteria for society on what “interest” is or should be, it is necessary to seek the contributions of economists and other social scientists.” (Diyanet-3).*

On the other hand, who are the most competent on religious matters? Certainly those people with appropriate knowledge and experience in religious fields! In this context, to determine whether the "ideas" of economists comply with Islamic tenets should be the responsibility of the Islamic scholars. Thus, society would benefit more if the "competent" economists cooperate with the "competent" Islamic scholars on economic matters.

In short: **Every job, including economics, should be carried out by those who are most competent**.

Are the Islamic economists capable of developing alternative scientific economic theories compatible with Western economic theories that can encompass both Muslim and non-Muslim societies?

Why not?

Do they have lesser Allah-given mental skills and abilities than their Western minded counterparts?

Surely not!

Bibliography

Internet sources

The Holy Book of Islam
http://www.islamicity.com/mosque/SURA1.HTM 2013-10-01
http://unitedamericanmuslim.org/english/2.html 2013-11-29

Diyanet "*İlmihâl*"
http://sorusor.diyanet.gov.tr/fmi/xsl/fetva/y_dokumcevap.xsl?-db=FetvaVT&-lay=wfkweb&-recid=1027&-find= 2012-09-19

Diyanet-1 Department of Religious Affairs, Koran in Turkish.
www.diyanet.gov.tr/kuran/Kuran_Meali/KURAN.pdf 2010-08-09

Diyanet-2 Department of Religious Affairs
https://kurul.diyanet.gov.tr/SoruSor/DiniKavramlarSozlugu.aspx 2013-11-08

Diyanet-3 Department of Religious Affairs – Ilmihal,
http://sorusor.diyanet.gov.tr/fmi/xsl/fetva/y_dokumcevap.xsl?-db=FetvaVT&-lay=wfkweb&-recid=1027&-find= 2010-08-09

Diyanet-4 ISAM- Islamic Encyclopeadia
http://www.tdvia.org/index.php 2014-01-28.

Kütub'u Sitte Hadisleri http://e-hadis.net/kutubu-sitte/bey(alimsatim)/1 2013-10-17

40 Hadith Qutsi http://www.usc.edu/org/cmje/religious-texts/hadith/qudsi.php 2013-10-17

500 Hadith http://foreninger.uio.no/mss/tr/hadith/hadith1.html#INTRO2HAD 2013-10-17

http-1 http://tdk.org.tr/tdksozluk/sozara.htm; 2006-12-18.

http-2 http://web.worldbank.org/WBSITE/EXTERNAL/DATASTATISTICS/EXTDECSTAMAN/0,,contentMDK:20878918~menuPK:2648303~page PK:64168445~piPK:64168309~theSitePK:2077967,00.html; 2006-10-09.

http-3 www.foreigntrade.gov.tr/ead/ekonomi/sayi7/kuresel.htm; 2007-01-16.

http-4 Post-Autistic Economics Review, www.paecon.net; 2007-02-05

http-5 http://encyclopedia2.thefreedictionary.com/Natural+Sciences 2013-10-16).

http-6 Islam in Concept http://d1.islamhouse.com/data/en/ih_books/single/en_Islam_in_Concept.pdf 2013-10-10

http-7 http://e-hadis.net/hadis-ara/tum-hadisler/hurma,-eşit-değiş-tokuş/6 2013-07-13.

http-8 http://www.islamicity.com/mosque/QURAN/43.htm 2013-07-20.

http-9 http://www.questionsonislam.com/article/questions-commercial-ethics 2013-10-18.

http-10 http://www.islamicity.com/mosque/QURAN/62.htm 2013-10-19

http-11 Encyclopaedia of Islam. http://referenceworks.brillonline.com/browse/encyclopaedia-of-islam-2/alphaRange/Rh%20-%20Rn/R 2013-12-01

http-12 Questions on Islam www.questionsonislam.com/article/what-interest-and-why-it-forbidden 2013-11-08

http-13	Riba (Faiz) http://errahman.de/modules.php?name=Encyclopedia&op= content&tid=1158 2013-11-09
http-14	*"Ribel fadl denilen faiz türü nedir? Günümüzde bu faiz nasıl gerçekleşir? Bir cep telefonunu iki cep telefonu ile değiştirmek faiz sayılır mı?"* www.sorularlaislamiyet.com/article/12775/ribel-fadl-denilen-faiz-turu-nedir-gunumuzde-bu-faiz-nasil-gerceklesir-bir-cep-telefonunu-iki-cep-telefonu-ile-degistirmek-faiz-sayilir-mi.html 2013-11-09
http-15	Dini Sözlük www.kuranikerim.com/dini_sozluk/ds_k3.htm#1621 2013-11-18
http-16	http://wol.jw.org/en/wol/d/r1/lp-e/1200002183 2013-11-14
http-17	http://www.islam-fyi.com/islamic-words/ribawiyy 2014-01-09

AbuSuleyman, A.A.	1989	*"The Theory of the Economics of Islam (II)"* **Journal of Ec. and Management**, 1998, Vol.6 No:2 www.iium.edu.my/enmjournal/vol6no2.pdf 2012-11-15, 87
Abozaid, A.	2013	*"Role of Fiqh in Islamic Finance"* Islam Iktisadı Atölyesi-1, 2-3 Mart-2013, Istanbul.
Acar, G.T.	2008	İktisadı Değiştirmek İletişim Yayınları, İstanbul.
Adamson, P. - R.C.Taylor	2008	İslam Felsefesine Giriş Küre Yayınları, İstanbul.
Agü, S.O.S.	1989	*"Rationality in Economic Theory"* **Journal of Islamic Economics**, 1989, Vol.2 No:1, 79 www.iium.edu.my/enmjournal/vol2no1.pdf 2012-11-15
Ahmad, A.- Mannan, M.A.- Kahf, M. (Eds.)	1992	*"Int. Economic Relations From Islamic Perspective"* Islamic Development Bank, IRTI www.irtipms.org/PubAllE.asp, 2013-10-22
Ahmed, H. (Ed.)	2002	Theoretical Foundations of Islamic Economics Islamic research & Training Inst., Islamic Dev. Bank a-Yousri,A. Methodological Approach to Islamic Ec.20 b- Khan,M.F. Fiqh Foun. of Theory of Islamic Ec. 61 c- Al-Jarhi,M.A. Transactions in Coven.&Islamic Ec.89 d- Hallaq,S. Indıvidual, Society, & Social Choice in Islamic Thought, 103

		e- Ahmed, H. Analytical Tools of Islamic Ec., 123 f- Baldwin,K. & et.al. On Determining Moral Hazard and Adverse Selection in the Islamic Firm, 145 g- Z.Iqbal, Portfolio Choices&Asset Pricing in Islamic Framework, 167
Akar, M.	2008	Tüketim Ahlâkı ve İsraf Diyanet Yayınları, 776, Ankara.
--- " ---	2008	İş ve Ticaret Ahlâkı Diyanet Yayınları, 730, Ankara.
Akın, C.	1986	Faizsiz Bankacılık ve Kalkınma Kayıhan Yayınları, Ankara.
Altuğ, T.	1996	İslam Ekonomisi Üzerine Karakoç, Yayınları.
Altıntaş, H.	1985	İbn Sina Metafiziği A.Ü. İlahiyat Fakültesi Yay. No:177
Ariff, M.	1989	"*Islamic Banking in Malaysia*" **Journal of Islamic Economics**, 1989, Vol.2 No:1, 67 www.iium.edu.my/enmjournal/vol2no1.pdf 2012-11-15
Armağan, S.	2005	İslam Ekonomisi Gündönümü Yayınları, Istanbul.
Aruç, N.Y.	2004	İbn Rüşd'ün Eğitim Felsefesi Rağbet Yayınları, Istanbul.
--- " ---	2007	İbn Rüşd'ün Felsefi Düşüncesi Rağbet Yayınları, Istanbul.
Ashker, A.- Wilson, R.	2006	"*Islamic Economics: A Short History*" www.bandung2.co.uk/Books/Files/Economics/Islamic%20 Economics%20%28A%20Short%20 History%29.pdf, 2012-11-15
Atay, H.	1974	Farabi ve İbn Sina'ya göre Yaratma Ankara Üniversitesi
Ayasbeyoğlu, N.	1955	İbn Rüşd'ün Felsefesi A.Ü. İlahiyat Fakültesi.
Aydın, E.	2008	İslamiyetin Ekonomi Politiği Kırmızı Yayınları, Istanbul.
Ayni, M.A.	2011	Gazali İnsan Yayınları, Istanbul.
Bahari, Z. - Wahbalbari, A.	2013	"Islamic Economics Assumption Revisited: Contemplating of the Concept of Scarcity" İslam İktisadı Atölyesi-1, 2-3 Mart-2013, Istanbul.
Bakhtiari, S. - et. al.	2010	"*Income Distribution & Economic Growth*" **Journal of Third World Studies,** Vol. XXVn, No. 2, EBSCO Database, 2012-10-31

Bayındır, A.	2007	"*Ticaret ve Faiz*" **Süleymaniye Vakfı Yayınları**, Istanbul www.suleymaniyevakfi.org 2012-12-26
--- " ---	2009	"**İslam Fıkhı Açısından Borçlanmalarda Enflasyon Farkı**" www.suleymaniyevakfi.org/arastirmalar/islam-fikhi-acisindan-borclanmalarda-enflasyon-farki.html 2013-11-17
Bayraktar, M.	2007	İslam'da Bilim ve Teknoloji Tarihi Diyanet Vakfı Yayınları: 30, Ankara.
Bayram, M.	2008	Seçuklular Zamanında Konya'da Dini ve Fikri Hareketler. NKM yayınları: 58, Istanbul.
--- " ---	2009	Danışmend Oğulları Devletinin Bilimsel ve Kültürel Mirası, Yayınevi yok, yazarın kendi yayını.
Bediüzzaman	S.Nursi (...)	"İktisat Risalesi" http://www.bediuzzamansaidnursi.org/icerik/iktisad-risalesi 2014-01-18
Behdad, S.	2005	"*Revolutionary Surge & Quiet Demise of Islamic Ec. in Iran*" www.international.ucla.edu/cms/files/behdadtxt.pdf 2012-11-15
Bircan, H.H.	2008	İslam Felsefesine Giriş Ensar Neşriyat, Istanbul.
Bjorvatn, K.	1998	"*Islamic Economics and Economic Development*" www.globalwebpost.com/farooqm/study_res/ i_econ_fin/bjorvatn_islamic_econ.pdf, 2012-11-15
Blaug, M.	1990	The History of Economic Thought Edward Elgar Pub.. Ltd., Hants
Boer, T.J.	1960	İslamda Felsefe Tarihi Balkanoğlu Matbaacılık, Ankara, Çev. Y. Kutluay
Bolay, S.H.	1993	Aristo Metafiziği ile Gazali Metafiziğinin Karşılaştırılması, MEB Yayınları: 500
Bozdağ, İ.	1991	İnsanlığın Son Çerçevesi: üçüncü çözüm Emre Yayınları, Istanbul.
Caldwell, B.J.	1994	Beyond Positivism: Economic Methodology in the 20th Century. Routledge, London.
Cassidy, J.	1996	The Decline of Economics The New Yorker, December 2.
Chapra, M.U.	2001-a	What is Islamic Economics? Prize Winners' Lecture Serie 9 Islamic research & Training Inst. Islamic Dev. Bank

--- " ---	2001-b	"*Islamic Economic Thought & The New Global Ec.*" http://www.irti.org/irj/go/km/docs/documents/IDBDevelopments/Internet/English/IRTI/CM/downloads/IES_Articles/Vol%209-1..M%20U%20Chapra..ISLAMIC%20ECONOMIC%20THOUGHT.pdf, 2012-11-04
--- " ---	2008	"*The Islamic Vision of Development in the Light of Maqasid al-Shari'ah, The Int.Institute of Islamic Thought*" http://i-epistemology.net/attachments/201_Omar-Chapra-Islamic-Development%5B1%5D.pdf 2012-11-15
--- " ---	2010	"*Islamic Economics: What It Is & How It Developed*" http://eh.net/encyclopedia/article/chapra.islamic 2012-11-04
Chapra, Ö. - et.al.	1991	İslam Ekonomisi ve Sosyal Güvenlik Sistemi Marifet yayınları: 46, Istanbul.
Choudry, M.A.	2013	"*Islamic Economic and Socio-Scientific Methodology...*" İslam İktisadı Atölyesi-1, 2-3 Mart-2013, Istanbul.
Cihan, A.K.	1998	İbn Sina ve Gazali'de Bilgi Problemi İnsan Yay., Istanbul.
Coase, R.H.	1991	Nobel Prize Lecture, Dec.1991, Stockholm.
Çakır, C.	2012	"*Batı ve İslam İktisat Düşüncesinde İnsan*" İslam ve Ekonomi Sempozyumu, I-II, İKDER.
Çarıkcı, E.	1989	Countertrade Policies & Prospect for Cooperation Among İslamic-Countries. TOBB Publ. No.136, Ankara.
Çızakça, M.	1998	"*Awqaf in History & its Implications for Modern Islamic Eco.*", **Islamic Ec. Studies**, Vol.6, No. 1 http://www.irti.org/irj/go/km/docs/documents/IDBDevelopments/Internet/English/IRTI/CM/downloads/IES_Articles/Vol%2061..Murat%20Cizakca..AWQAF%20IN%20HISTORY%20AND%20ITS%20IMPLICATIONS.pdf, 2012-11-04
Çobanoğlu, Ş.	2013	İslam Ekonomisi Yediveren, Istanbul.
Çubukçu, İ.A.	1989	Gazzali ve Şüphecilik A.Ü. İlahiyat Fakültesi Yay. No:188
Demir, Ö. (Ed.)	1999	İslam, Sivil Toplum, Piyasa Ekonomisi Liberte Yayınları, Ankara.
Demir, M.	2006	İslam Devletleri Tarihi: 622-1599 Değişim Yayınları, Istanbul.
Dermenghem, E.	2006	Hazreti Muhammed'in Hayatı Alkım Yayınevi, Istanbul.

Durî, A.	1991	İslam İktisat Tarihine Giriş Endülüs Yayınları, Istanbul.
Düzdağ, E.	2012	Ebussuud Efendi Fetvaları Kapı Yayınları, Istanbul.
Ekinci, Y.	2008	Ahilik Ankara
Erdoğdu, S.	1994	İslam Ekonomisinde Gelir ve Sermaye Sebil Yayınları: 200, Istanbul.
Eskicioğlu, O.	1979	İslam Ekonomisinde Gelir Dağılımı Atatürk Üni., İslami İlimler Fakültesi
--- " ---	1983	İslam Açısından Enflasyon ve Çözüm Yolları www.enfal.de/enflasyon.pdf 2013-04-09
--- " ---	1999	İslam ve Ekonomi www.enfal.de/islamekonomi.pdf 2013-04-09
Evliya Çelebi	2004	Seyahatname (Gördüklerim) Kabalcı, İsyanbul.
Foul, B.E.- Soliman, B.	2006	"*The Economic Role of the State*" EBSCO Database, 2012-10-31
Friedman, M.	1953	On the Methodology of Positive Economics
Garaudy,R.- Bercavi, F.	2012	İslamiyet ve Sosyalizm. Rebeze Kitaplığı, Istanbul. Çev. H. Erdem.
Ghazali, Imam	2007	Dilimize Nasıl Sahip Çıkabiliriz? Polen Yayınları, Istanbul.
--- " ---	2008	Yöneticilere Tavsiyeler İlke Yayıncılık, Istanbul.
--- " ---	2009	Dünyanın Süsüne Aldanma Dua Yayıncılık, Istanbul.
--- " ---	2011-a	Kudsi Hadisler Semerkand-58.
--- " ---	2011-b	Hakikate Giden Yol Semerkand-54
--- " ---	(…)	Âbidler Yolu Hisar Yayınevi, Istanbul.
Ghazali, A.H.	1994	Man is the Basis of the Islamic Strategy for Ec. Development Islamic Research & Training Inst. Islamic Dev. Bank.
Ghazanfar, S.M.- Islahi, A.A.	(..)	"*Economic Thought of Al-Ghazali*" **Islamic Research Series**, King Abdulaziz Uni.-2 http://islamiccenter.kau.edu.sa/english/Publications/Islahi/Economics%20Thought%20of%20Al-Ghazali.pdf, 2012-11-04
Gökalp, M.F – Turan,G.	1993	İslam Toplumunun Ekonomik Yapısı Faisal Eğitim ve Yardımlaşma Vakfı, Istanbul.

Gülen, F. 2009 "*Faiz Meselesi*"
http://tr.fgulen.com/content/view/17262/3/, 2013-11-14

Güler, Z. 2012 40 Hadiste İş ve Ticaret Ahlâkı
İGİAD Yayınları: 9, Istanbul.

Günenç, H. (…) İslam'da Ticaret
Faisal Finans Kurumu, Kültür yayınları: 4

Gürak, H. 2007 "*Kutsal İdeolojinin Eleştirisi*"
www.hasmendi.net 2013-01-18

--- " --- 2012 Heterodox Economics
Peter Lang, Frankfurt.

--- " --- 2013 Heterodox Economics-2
Peter Lang, Frankfurt.

Gürkan, S.L. 2009 "*Bir Dinler Tarihi Yorumcusu Olarak İbn Haldun*"
EKEV Akademi Dergisi, Yıl:13, Sayı:39

Haddad, L. 1977 "*A Fourteenth-Century Theory of Ec. Growth & Development*"
Kyklos, Vol. 30, 1977, Fasc.2, 195-213.

Halebi, İ. 2011 Mülteka Tercümesi
Yasin Yayınevi, Istanbul. Çev. H. Vanlıoğlu.

Han, M.E. 1988 İslam Ekonomisinin Temel Meseleleri
Kayıhan Yayınevi, Istanbul.

Haneef, M.A.- Furqani, H. (…) "*Contemporary Islamic Economics*"
www.academia.edu/992875/Contemporary_Islamic_Economics_The_Missing_Dimension_of_Genuine_Islamization, 2012-11-04

Harris, D.J. 1978 Capital Accumulation and Income Distribution
Routledge & Kegan Paul, London.

Harrod, R.F. 1937 "*Mr. Keynes and Traditional Theory*"
Econometrica, Vol.5; No.1, Jan. 74-86

----- " ----- 1973 Economic Dynamics.
Macmillan Press, London.

Hasan, Z. 1995 "*Economics Develeopment in Islamic Perspective*"
Journal of Islamic Economics, 1995, Vol.3 No:2
www.iium.edu.my/enmjournal/vol3no2.pdf 2012-11-15

--- " --- 1998 "*Islamization of Knowledge*"
Journal of Ec. and Management, 1998, Vol.6 No:2
www.iium.edu.my/enmjournal/vol6no2.pdf 2012-11-15

--- " --- 2008 "*Theory of Profit from Islamic Perspective*"
http://mpra.ub.uni-muenchen.de/8129/ 2012-10-25.

Hassan, A. 2013 "*What is the Current* Situation of Islamic Economics Studies Today and What is the Future of Them"
İslam İktisadı Atölyesi-1, 2-3 Mart-2013, Istanbul.

Hızlı, M.	2008	"*Osmanlı Medreselerinde Okutulan Dersler ve Eserler*" UÜ, İlahiyat Fakültesi Dergisi, Cilt.17, Sayı.1, 25-46
Hicks, J. R.	1983	Classics and Moderns. Basil Blackwell Publ., Oxford.
Hodgson, G.M.	2004	"*On the Problem of Formalism in Economics*" **Post-Autistic Economics Review**; issue no. 28)
Hoover, G.E.	2008	"*The Present State of Economic Science*" **Econ Journal Watch**; Vol.5; No.3; 2008-10-12 www.econjournalwatch.org/pdf/HooverCharacter IssuesSeptember2008.pdf
Ibn Haldun	2012	"*Mukaddime'den*" İş Ahlakı Dergisi, Mayıs-2012, Cilt:5, Sayı:9, 177-184
Ibn Sinâ	2012	En-Necât Kabalcı, Istanbul, Çev. K. Şenel
Ihsanoğlu, E.	1996	Büyük Cihad'dan Frenk Fodulluğuna Iletişim Yayıncılık, Istanbul.
--- " ---	2010	Osmanlılar ve Bilim Etkileşim Yayınları, Istanbul.
Iqbal, M.	1998	"*Organization of Production*" in Kahf, "Lessons in Islamic Economics; 1998, Vol.-2; 399
Iqbal, M.- Ali, S.S.- Muljawan, D. (Eds)	2007	"*Advances in Islamic Economics and Finance*" (Vol.1) Islamic Development Bank, IRTI www.irtipms.org/PubText/230.pdf, 2013-10-22
Irmiş, A.	2008	"*Küreselleşme Sürecinde Yeni Gelişen Piyasalar ve KOBİler*" www.hasmendi.net, 2008-01-14.
Islahi, A.A.	1997	"*History of Economic Thought in Islam: a Bibliography*" http://islamiccenter.kau.edu.sa/english/Publications/ Islahi/HISTORY%20OF%20ECONOMIC%20 THOUGHT%20IN%20ISLAM.pdf, 2012-11-04
Kahf, M.	1989	"*Zakat: Unresolved Issues in the Contemporary Fiqh*" **Journal of Islamic Economics**, 1989, Vol.2 No:2 www.iium.edu.my/enmjournal/vol2no2.pdf 2012-11-15
--- " --- (Ed)	1998	Lessons in Islamic Economics, Vol. 1 &2 IRTI, Islamic Development Bank
--- " ---	2013-a	"*Islamic Economics, what Went Wrong?*" www.iefpedia.com/english/wpcontent/uploads/ 2009/11/Islamic-Economics-What-Went-Wrong.pdf 2013-05-08
--- " ---	2013-b Realism	http://monzer.kahf.com/papers/english/Realism.pdf, 2013-10-10
--- " ---	2013-c	Islamic Economics: Notes on Definition and Methodology http://monzer.kahf.com/papers/english/ paper_of_methdology.pdf, 2013-10-10

Karaman, H.	2012	"*Faiz hakkında soruya yanıt*" www.hayrettinkaraman.net/sc/00144.htm 2012-09-19
Karim, W.J.	2012	"The Economic Crisis, Capitalism and Islam" **Globalizations,** March–June 2010, Vol.7, 105–125 EBSCO Database, 2012-10-31
Kaya, M.	2010	İslam Filozoflarından Felsefe Metinleri Klasik Yayınları, Istanbul
Kaymakçı, Ö.B.	2012	"*Seküler Bir Alan Olarak İktisat ve Din İlişkisi*" İnsan ve Toplum, Cilt:2, Sayı:4
Keynes, J.M.	1973	The General Theory of Employment, Interest and Money The Macmillan Press, London.
Khan, F.	2013	"*Where Islamic Economics Should Generate*" İslam İktisadı Atölyesi-1, 2-3 Mart-2013, Istanbul.
Khan, F.	1998-a	"*Investment Demand Function in Profit-Loss Sharing Based System*" in Kahf, "Lessons in Islamic Economics; 1998, Vol.-1; 313
--- " ---	1998-b	"*Growth Stability and Inflation in an Islamic Macro Framework*" in Kahf, "Lessons in Islamic Economics; 1998, Vol.-1; 333
--- " ---	2013	"*Where Islamic Economics Should Generate*" İslam İktisadı Atölyesi-1, 2-3 Mart-2013, İstanbul.
Khan, M.A.	[..]	"*Islamic Economics: The State of the Art*" http://i-epistemology.net/attachments/530_IOD%20-%20VII%20-%20Islamic%20Economics%20-%20The%20State%20of%20the%20Art.pdf, 2012-11-15
Koca, F.	2008	Molla Hüsrev Diyanet Vakfı Yayınları, Ankara.
Korkmaz, C.H.	2012	"*Bir Davranış ve Örgütlenme Modeli Olarak Tüccar Ahlakı*" İş Ahlakı Dergisi, Mayıs-2012, Cilt:5, Sayı:9, 37-60
Korkmaz, A. & et. al.	2013	İnsani Ücret İLKE Araştırma Raporları:3, Istanbul.
Kozak, İ.E.	2012	"İbn Haldun'un İşletme ve Kamu Yönetimine İlişkin *Görüşlerine Günümüzden Bir Bakış*". İş Ahlakı Dergisi, Mayıs-2012, Cilt:5, Sayı:9, 163-176
Köse, S.	2012	İslâm İş ve Ticaret Ahlâkı İGİAD Yayınları: 12, Istanbul.
Kuran, T.	1995	"*Islamic Economics and the Islamic Subeconomy*" http://econ.duke.edu/uploads/assets/People/Kuran/Islamic%20economics%20and%20Islamic%20subeconomy.pdf, 2012-11-15

--- " ---	1997	"*The Genesis of Islamic Economics*" **Social Research**, Vol.64, No:2 EBSCO Database, 2012-10-31
--- " ---	2010	"*Orta Doğu'daki Ekonomik Azgelişmişliğin Kurumsal"Kökenleri*" http://econ.duke.edu/uploads/assets/People/Kuran/Kayseri%20talk%20(2010).pdf, 2012-11-02
--- " ---	2012-a	"*The Economic Roots of Political Underdevelopment in the Middle East*", Sothern Economic Journal, 2012, 78 http://econ.duke.edu/uploads/media_items/kuran-se-association-lecture-2011.original.pdf, 2012-11-02
--- " ---	2012-b	Yollar Ayrılırken: Ortadoğu'nun Geri Kalma Sürecinde İslam Hukukunun Rolü (The Long Divergence) Yapı Kredi Yayınları, Çev. N.Elhüsyni
Kuran,T.- Lucas, R.	1988	"*On The Mechanics Of Economic Development*" **Journal Of Monetary Economics**, July, 1988,342
Lustig, S.	2012	"*Judicial Biases in Ottoman Istanbul*" http://econ.duke.edu/uploads/media_items/kuran-lustig-paper-on-islamic-courts.original.pdf, 2012-11-02
Kutluer, İ.	1998	Akıl ve İtikad İz Yayıncılık, İstanbul.
Mannan, M.A.	(…)	İslam Ekonomi Toplumunun Kuruluşu Fikir Yayınları, Istanbul. Çev. A. Saidoğlu.
--- " ---	2013	"İslam'da Tüketim İlkeleri" (Çev.B.Zengin-T.Ömeroğlu) http://islamekonomisi.org/islamda-tuketim-ilkeleri/ 2013-04-13
Marshall, A.	1990	Principle of Economics, Vol. 1 & 2 Macmillan And Co., London.
Marx, K.	1976	Capital, Vol. I Penguin Books
Metwally, M.A.	(…)	"*A behavioral Model of an Islamic Firm*" Center for Research in Islamic Economics. King Abdulaziz Uni. Jeddah, Research Series No:5
Mouhammed, A.H.	2008	"*On Ibn Khaldun's Critique of the Market Economy With Some Lessons to the Arab World*" **Journal of Third World Studies**, Vol. XXV, No:2
Muqorobin, M.	2012	"*Journey of Islamic Economics in the Modern World*" http://islamiccenter.kau.edu.sa/7iecon/English/Englisg%20Papers/%5B27%5D%20Masyhudi%20Muqorobin.pdf, 2012-11-04
Neccar, A.	1978	İslam Ekonomisine Giriş Hilal Yayınları, Istanbul. Çev. R. Nazlı

Nisar, K. 2010 "*The Role of Venture Capital Model in an Islamic Ec.System*" www.eurekahedge.com/news/10_Jul_IFN_The_Role_of Venture_Capital_Model_in_Islamic_Economic_ System.asp, 2012-11-16

Orman, S. 2007 Gazali'nin İktisat Felsefesi İnsan yayınları, Istanbul

--- " --- 2008 İktisadi Kalkınma Politikaları ve Değerler in: R.Şentürk (Ed.) 2008, Ekonomik Kalkınma ve Değerler, UTESAV Yayınları, Istanbul.

--- " --- 2010 İktisat, Tarih ve Toplum Küre Yayınları, Istanbul

--- " --- 2013-a "*İslam, İnsan ve İktisat*" www.ikder.org/sempozyum/makaleler/Sabri_Orman-Islam_Ekonomisi_Kavrami.pdf, 2013-02-20

--- " --- 2013-b Gazali : Biyografisi, Hakikat Araştırması, Felsefe Eleştirisi, İhya Hareketi, Etkisi. İnsan Yayınları, Istanbul.

Ökte, M.K.S. 2010 "*Fundamentals of Islamic Ec. & Finance: Th. & Practice*" **Electronic Journal of Social Sciences**, 2010 C.9 31 EBSCO Database, 2012-10-31

Özakıncı, C. 2010 İslamda Bilimin Yükselişi ve Çöküşü (827-1107) Otopsi Yayınları, Istanbul.

Özcan, E.S. 2005 İbn-i Sina Ötüken Neşriyat, Istanbul.

Özdemir, Ş. 2013-a "*İslami Sermaye ve Sınıf*" Çalışma İlişkileri Dergisi, http://www.calismailiskileridergisi.org, 2013-02-24

--- " --- 2013-b "*Din-Ekonomi İlişkisi ve Güncel Arayışlar*" dergi.ilahiyat.omu.edu.tr/DergiPdfDetay.aspx?ID=66 2013-02-24

--- " --- 2013-c "*Bir ‚İslam Ekonomisi' Nasıl Mümkün Olur?*" İslam İktisadı Atölyesi-1, 2-3 Mart-2013, Istanbul.

Özsoy, İ. 2006 "*Human Transformation in the Transition Economies: The Case of Georgia*" **Journal of East-West Business**, Vol. 12, No: 4

--- " --- 2009 "*İktisadi Adamdan Toplum Adamına*" **Bilig**, 2009, Sayı: 48, 177-206

--- " --- 2013-a "*Toplum Adamından Müslüman Adama*" Çerçeve, 2013, Sayı: 60, 12-27

--- " --- 2013-b "*Why Did the Vatican Suggest Islamic Finance?*" www.todayszaman.com/news-307052-why-did-the-vatican-suggest-islamic-financeby-ismail-ozsoy-.html, 2013-03-14

Rahman, F.	1995	*"Islam and the Problem of Economic Justice"* **Journal of Islamic Economics**, 1995, Vol.3 No:2 www.iium.edu.my/enmjournal/vol3no2.pdf 2012-11-15,
Ricardo, D.	1990	On The Principles Of Political Economy And Taxation, Cambridge Uni. Press
Robinson, J.	1962	Economic Philosophy.
Romer, P.	1990	*"Endogenous Technological Change"* **Journal Of Pol. Economy**, Vol.98, October.
--- " ---	1994	Comments, on G.Dosi & S. Fabiani, in **Silverberg,** G. – L. **Soete,(Eds) (1994)** **The Ec. Of Growth & Technical Change**. Edward Elgar Publ.
Rosly, S.A.	1995	*"Economic Principles in Islam"* **Journal of Islamic Economics**, 1995, Vol.3 No:2 www.iium.edu.my/enmjournal/vol3no2.pdf 2012-11-15,
Sadeq, A.H.M.	1989	*"Factor Pricing & Income Distr. from an Islamic Perspective"* **Journal of Islamic Economics**, 1989, Vol.2 No:2 www.iium.edu.my/enmjournal/vol2no2.pdf 2012-11-15
Sadr, M.B.	1980	İslam Ekonomi Doktrini (*Iqtisaduna* - Our [Islamic] Economics), Hicret Yayınları
Salahuddin, A.	1998	International Economic Relations and Order in an Islamic Perspective. in Kahf, "Lessons in Islamic Economics; 1998, Vol.-2; 575
Salleh, M.S.	2013	*"Concepts in Islamic Economics Revisited: The Case of Poverty"* İslam İktisadı Atölyesi-1, 2-3 Mart-2013, Istanbul.
Samuelson, P.	1973	The Samuelson Sampler. Thomas Horton & Co. New Jersey
Sarwath, L.	2013	*"Political Economy of Institutionalism"* İslam İktisadı Atölyesi-1, 2-3 Mart-2013, Istanbul.
Sayar, A.G.	2009	Osmanlı İktisat Düşüncesinin Çağdaşlaşması. Ötüken, Ankara.
Sayyid, T.	1989	*"Toward a Theory of Aggregate Output, Income, & Economic Inequalities Determination in an Islamic Economy"* **Journal of Islamic Economics**, 1989, Vol.2 No:1, 95 www.iium.edu.my/enmjournal/vol2no1.pdf 2012-11-15
Schumpeter, J.A.	1954	History of Economic Analysis Oxford Uni. Press, New York
Shahid E.M.	2013	**"İslâmî Finansın Sınırları: Eleştirel Bir Perspektif"** (Frontiers in Islamic Finance: A Critical Perspective) www.bisav.org.tr/yayinlar.aspx?module=makale&yayinid=116&menuID=3_3&yayintipid=3&makaleid=884 2013-11-09

Skousen, M. 2003 Modern İktisadın İnşası
(The Making of Modern Economics)
Liberte Yayınları, Ankara.

Solow, R. 1987 Nobel Prize Lecture,
Dec. 1987, Stockholm.

Stiglitz, J.E. 1999 Annual World Bank Conference on Dev. Economics

Suwailem, S. 2006 "*Hedging in Islamic Finance*"
Occasional Paper: 10, Islamic Development Bank

--- " --- 2008 Islamic Economics in a Complex World
Islamic Development Bank.

Şeraiti, A. 2004 İslam Ekonomisi (Shariati, A.)
Dünya yayınları, İstanbul. Çev. K. Çamurcu.

Tabakoğlu, A. 2008 İslam İktisadına Giriş
Dergah Yayınları, İstanbul.

--- " --- 2010 "İslam İktisat Ahlakı"
Din ve Hayat, İstanbul Müftülüğü Dergisi,
Sayı:10,s.18-22

--- " --- 2012 "*İktisat Öznesi Olarak İnsan*"
İslam ve Ekonomi Sempozyumu, I-II, İKDER.

Tabakoğlu, A- & et. al. 1988 İslam İktisadi Araştırmaları
Dergah Yayınları, Istanbul.

Tahir, S. 1998 "*Distribution in Islam*"
in Kahf, "Lessons in Islamic Economics; 1998, Vol.-2; 425

Timur, T. 1994 Osmanlı Kimliği
Hil Yayın, Istanbul.

Türker, M. 1956 Üç Tehafüt Bakımından Felsefe ve Din Münasebeti
A.Ü. Dil ve Tarih-Coğrafya Fak. Yay. 102, Ankara.

Uğur, A. 1982 Lütfi Paşa: Asafname
Kültür ve Turizm Bakanlığı Yay. 500, Ankara.

Uludağ, S. 2004 Felsefe-Din İlişkileri
Dergah Yayınları, Istanbul.

Umut, Ç. 2009-a İbni Sina
Demirbaş Yay., Istanbul.

--- " --- 2009-b Farabi
Demirbaş Yay., Istanbul.

Ülgener, S. 2006-a İktisadi Çözülmenin Ahlak ve Zihniyet Dünyası
Derin Yayınları, Istanbul.

--- " --- 2006-b Zihniyet ve Din: İslam
Derin Yayınları, Istanbul

Vernon, R. 1966 "*International Investment and International Trade in the Product Cycle*";
The Quarterly Journal of Economics; Vol.80; No.2,
190-207.

Yaş, M.	2013	“*Methodology of Islamic Eco: Seeking the Right Path*” İslam İktisadı Atölyesi-1, 2-3 Mart-2013, Istanbul.
Yeldan, E.	2013	Cumhuriyet Gazetesi, 20-Kasım-2013
Yousri, A.	2013	“Islamic Economics: Its Philosophy, Methodology, and Theoretical Construction.” İslam İktisadı Atölyesi-1, 2-3 Mart-2013, Istanbul.
Yücel, R. – Çiftçi, G.E.	2012	“*İş Görenin İş Etiği Tutum ve Davranış Algısı*” İş Ahlakı Dergisi, Mayıs-2012, Cilt:5, Sayı:9, 131-150
Zaman, S.M.H.	1984	“*Definition of Islamic Economics*” J. **Res. Islamic Econ.**, Vol. 1, No. 2, 49-50 (1404/1984) http://islamiccenter.kau.edu.sa/arabic/Magallah/Pdf/Old-1-2/SMZaman_16.pdf, 2012-11-16
Zaman, A.	2010	“*The Normative Foundations of Scarcity*” https://docs.google.com/viewer?a=v&pid=sites&srcid=ZGVmYXVsdGRvbWFpbnx6YW1hbmlzbGFtaWNlY29ufGd4OjY3Nzk4N2Y5OTlhYzc1NmY, 2012-11-16
--- ” ---	2013	“*Re-Defining Islamic Economics*” İslam İktisadı Atölyesi-1, 2-3 Mart-2013, Istanbul.
Zarqa, M.A.	1998	“*Consumer Behavior in an Islamic Economy*” in Kahf, “Lessons in Islamic Economics; 1998, Vol.-1; 371
Zerrinkub, A.	2005	İmam Gazali’nin Hayatı Ağaç Yayınları, Istanbul.

www.ingramcontent.com/pod-product-compliance
Ingram Content Group UK Ltd.
Pitfield, Milton Keynes, MK11 3LW, UK
UKHW021832100926
8556IPUK00004B/303